MANCHESTER'S
LOST DISTRICT

Life before the Arndale

Dickinson's Court 1969, looking towards Palace Street.

MANCHESTER'S
LOST DISTRICT
Life before the Arndale

KEITH WARRENDER
INTRODUCTION BY CHRIS MAKEPEACE

Willow
PUBLISHING

Willow Publishing
36 Moss Lane, Timperley
Altrincham, Cheshire WA15 6SZ

ISBN 978-0-946361-47-2

Book designed by Keith Warrender
Printed by the Buxton Press

Dedicated to Joseph George Warrender

New Brown Street c1900

CONTENTS

The area of the 'Lost District' now covered by the Manchester Arndale which was built in phases between 1972 and 2006.

Keith Warrender

FOREWORD

For many readers, the Manchester Arndale will have been there all their lives, but others may remember the area before the construction of this huge shopping centre. The old district could be described as 'Dickensian' with its dark narrow streets, squares, passageways and courts in this rather run-down part of the city centre. Huge warehouses and other commercial properties from the days of Manchester's growth as a great textile centre loomed over a street network which was largely unchanged from the late 1700s. You had merely to take a few steps off Market Street or one of the other main thoroughfares and you were in a bygone age.

It was an area that few people seemed to enter except as a cut-through to Cannon Street or towards Victoria Station. It came as no surprise when the Corporation decided that the old district was to be completely cleared for a much-needed shopping centre.

The 1968 public enquiry into the new development accepted there was much history associated with these old streets but it was agreed it should be swept away by the Corporation and the developers. Today, the Manchester Arndale is visited by millions of people each year who will be completely unaware of the fascinating stories of the people who once lived and worked in this thirteen-acres site I've entitled the 'Lost District'.

Below: Palace Street 1969, looking down Dickinson's Court. To the left of the archway is the boarded-up premises of Mancunian Textiles Ltd. On the right is the entrance to the former Stork Club.

Further along Dickinson's Court in the 1950s were Lomas and Baynes, printers, and Garden Vale, haircloth manufacturers. Compulsory Purchase Orders for the securing and redevelopment of the area were issued in 1970 and 1971.

Keith Warrender

Market Street, from the old Lewis's store in 1969.

Market Street.

Bust of industrialist and civic pioneer, Malcolm Ross, see page 97.

Even in its final years, the area was perhaps used more extensively than some will have realised. In addition to the many commercial businesses still in existence, people came to the boutiques, record shops and second-hand bookstalls. It had a thriving nightlife with coffee beat-clubs, cabaret clubs and pubs in the maze of back streets. One of Manchester's oldest pubs, 'The Seven Stars', had been controversially taken down many years before.

This book is an exploration of the 'Lost District' with a selection of some of the people and places of interest from over the centuries. Pubs and hotels feature strongly in it, not only because they were landmarks but because they were also places where key meetings took place as people fought for their rights of employment. They were also venues for business and political meetings, exhibitions, concerts and even visiting giants!

It was in this area where people demonstrated during food shortages, and where some of the great radical voices of the city published newspapers. Here, royalty was entertained and one of the best music hall artists, Harry Liston, owned a pub. I've devoted a chapter to his life and career because little has been written about him, and yet he was one of Manchester's finest-ever performers. Most shoppers at the Arndale will also be unaware they are walking over the sites of a former chapel, a graveyard, a private chapel, the premises of distinguished merchants, a pioneering cinema and so much more.

I've been interested in the area for many years, and took some photographs fifty years ago. This is the first time they have been published, and with hindsight I should have taken a lot more. However, Manchester Council

Keith Warrender

Finigan's store 31 Market Street 1969.

Keith Warrender

One of the few remnants
of the the 'Lost District' -
the shaft of Hyde's Cross
in the grounds of Chetham's
with a 1653 inscription.

have an extensive collection on their Manchester Images website. Since then I have acquired further photographs and I'm grateful to all those who have lent me images for this book.

With the exception of photographic records, it is unfortunate that apart from Hyde's Cross little else has been preserved from the site such as street signs, building name-plates and pub signs. Some were donated to museums but nothing is known of them today. However, if you know where to look in the Arndale, there is still in existence a hatch to a cable chamber on the site of the junction of former Cannon Street and New Brown Street.

There is just one plaque on the Arndale building which commemorates the Shudehill Fight. There ought to be others both on the outside and inside of the shopping centre celebrating the achievements of Manchester people. I hope this book brings back memories for some and gives everyone an insight into a part of Manchester which is lost for ever.

Helen Webster, who kindly lent me old photographs, remembered being taken around the the area when young, and seeing lots of the premises used by tailors who worked sitting cross-legged in dimly-lit basements. If you have recollections or photographs of the area, please let me know.

Keith Warrender

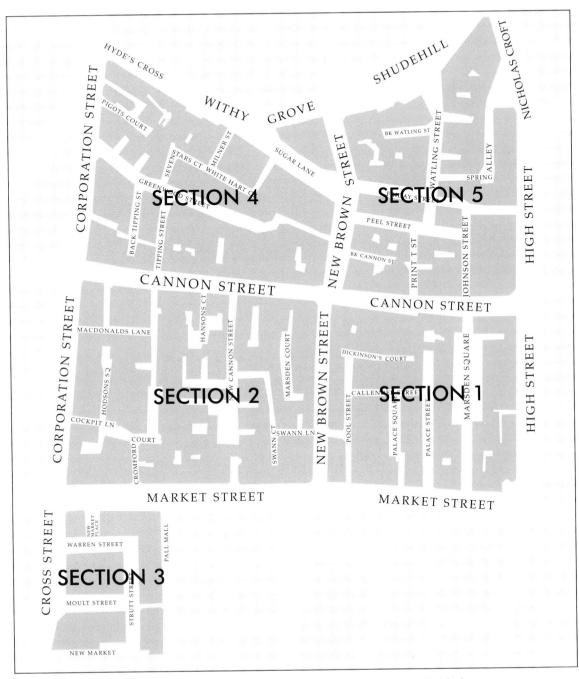

For the purposes of this book, the 'Lost District' is divided
into five sections based on the street network of an 1886 plan.

Keith Warrender

The re-constructed Roman fort at Castlefield.

INTRODUCTION

It is not certain when and where the first settlement took place in the area now covered by the modern City of Manchester, but around 74AD a Roman fort was constructed overlooking the confluence of the rivers Irwell and Medlock as a staging post between Chester and York. Around the fort, a civilian settlement developed whose residents met the needs of those based at the fort. However, it was not from this Roman settlement that the modern Manchester developed, but from a settlement that grew up about a mile east of the fort, on a sandstone bluff overlooking the Irk and the Irwell. The site appears to have had a third river along its eastern boundary, the River Dene, that flowed roughly along the line of Shudehill, Withy Grove and Cateaton Street. It was to this protected site that the parish church was re-located during the 8th or 9th centuries. After the Norman Conquest, the new landowners for the area, the Grelley family, built a small motte and bailey castle which was replaced after less than a century by a more domestic building which was known as the Manor House.

Manchester in the late 11th and early 12th centuries was little more than a large village with its buildings clustered around the parish church and the manor house. It was close to the parish church that an open area developed, ultimately becoming the Market Place. By the 14th century, there were several roads leading out of the Market Place including Old Millgate, Long Millgate, Deansgate, St Mary's Gate as well as Withy Grove and Shudehill, which are the only two roads from the mediaeval period today which form part of the perimeter of the Arndale Centre.

Little is known about mediaeval Manchester except that which can be gleaned from surviving documents. The area known as 'Manchester' was one of 30 townships that made up the parish of Manchester and was bounded by the rivers Medlock, Irk and Irwell and included what is today known as 'Ancoats'. In 1222 Manchester received a charter enabling an annual fair to be held on Acres Field (now St Ann's Square) for two days in September. This was later extended to three days in 1227. The importance of the village was further enhanced in 1301 when the Grelleys granted the residents a charter which laid down what they could and could not do. The charter was rescinded in 1359, but the principles laid down in it continued to provide the basis for the administration of local government in Manchester until the late 18th century.

It is not clear when Manchester began to develop in a southerly direction, along what is now called Market Street, then called Market Stede Lane. It has been suggested that Market Street came into existence in the early 16th century, but it may have been during the previous century. There was certainly a road in existence by 1552 when Market Street is mentioned in the surviving Court Leet records. There are references to the appointment of 'scavengers', whose job it was to ensure that property occupiers carried out their responsibilities in keeping the road in front of their properties clean. Later, 'bylawmen' were appointed to ensure that regulations made by the Court Leets were observed. All the roads and streets had similar officials appointed for

them at this time. It also known that there were problems with dung heaps being created in front of houses. Swine cotes and middens were also creating problems, but whether they were located at the rear of houses is not clear. Both Withy Grove and Shudehill had officials responsible for the state of these roads and enforcing the rules and regulations made by the Court Leet.

In order to carry off surface water, there was a ditch along the side of the road, which presumably terminated above the River Irwell, but there appears to have been a habit of throwing rubbish into it and creating a problem. Residents were ordered not to do this. On the side now covered by the Arndale Centre, from 1523, a wooden pipe was laid to carry water from the springs of Spring Gardens to a tank on the edge of the Market Place which was meant to enable residents to get fresh, clean water for domestic purposes, but this was not always the case. Other problems included the encroachment on the pavement and road, gradually reducing its width. Although attempts were made to prevent this, they appear to have had little effect so that by the

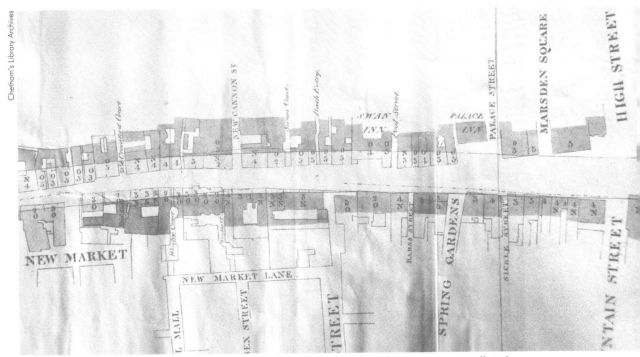

Chetham's Library Archives

1821 plan of the improvement scheme to substantially widen Market Street, with many properties affected.

late 18th century, Market Street was rather irregular in its width, leading to its widening in the 1820s. Further evidence of the existence of Market Street is provided by the fact that the ducking stool was relocated to the Daub Holes (now Piccadilly) in the early 17th century, which suggests there was a track leading in a southerly direction from the Market Place. The Daub Holes was the only place where residents could dig clay to repair their homes, although it is clear from the Court Leet records that some people were in the habit of digging up the road to obtain clay. There also appear to have been clay pits in the area, between what is now Market Street and Withy Grove as there is a reference to a clay pit in the area whilst at the top end of Market Street there is a reference to a 'Kiln Field'. Bricks were produced for the construction of chimneys.

In the mid-17th century Market Street was said to have been a narrow, tortuous thoroughfare with timber-framed houses, high peak gables and over-hanging roofs. Illustrations from the early 19th century confirm that this had not changed for a long time. During the siege of Manchester in September 1642 by Lord Strange, it was necessary to erect defences at the southerly end of the road as part of the town defences. Just over a century later, in 1745, Market Street saw the arrival of Bonnie Prince Charlie, who stayed at Mr Dickenson's house on Market Street.

As Manchester expanded during the latter half of the 18th century, the undeveloped land in the central area began to disappear under a sea of development. New roads were created to provide access to these developments whilst some of the existing roads began to assume more importance. During the latter half of the 18th century, Market Street became the main road from the centre of the town heading out in a southerly direction. Eventually it was connected with the Manchester to Buxton turnpike in Ardwick, providing an improved link to Stockport and further afield. The growing importance of Market Street resulted in its becoming increasingly congested, and dangerous for pedestrians. Traffic heading for the Market Place on market day mingled with stage-coaches and wagons.

Market Street c1820 with the Lower Swan coach office on the left, looking towards Piccadilly.

Chris Makepeace

The drawing illustrates the steepness of Market street and its narrowness looking down towards Deansgate, before the improvements in the 1820s.

Eventually, in the 1820s, action was taken to improve Market Street by widening it, rebuilding the properties on either side of the road and reducing the gradient to make it easier for both pedestrians and horse-drawn vehicles. The result was improved access between Piccadilly and the Market Place.

During the late 18th and early 19th centuries, several new streets were constructed in central Manchester. Amongst these was Peter Street, which enabled vehicles going to the canal basin at Castlefield or the quays on the River Irwell to avoid the congested route along Market Street and Deansgate. The improvements to Market Street also enabled Cross Street to be opened onto Market Street, improving access to the Town Hall on King Street. Other new roads in the 1830s and 1840s included Victoria Street, which was intended to make it easier for those who used Bury New Road to have better access to

the centre of Manchester, especially to Deansgate. In the 1840s, the construction of Corporation Street was started, providing an improved access to York Street (now Cheetham Hill Road). The construction of Corporation Street severed the area now covered by the Arndale Centre from the traditional centre of Manchester around the parish church, by now Manchester Cathedral, and the Market Place.

As Manchester grew, there was a gradual movement of population away from the central area. Market Street, Withy Grove and Shudehill were no exception to this. The new properties erected as a result of the improvements to Market Street were shops, offices and warehouses and did not include residential property, and even those residential properties that existed tended to be abandoned and became used for commercial purposes. As the 19th century progressed the whole of the area became increasingly congested

Chris Makepeace

Horse-drawn traffic at the congested corner of Market Street and Corporation Street. The site then in the occupation of Moss and Son was later destroyed by enemy bombing during the 1940 Blitz.

with traffic and pedestrians, especially business-men, those working and even shoppers. Amongst the businessmen, there were not only those from the United Kingdom, but many from abroad. Market Street and the surrounding area might be said to represent the cosmopolitan nature of Manchester and its trade.

The introduction of horse-drawn buses from the 1820s onwards increased the amount of traffic using Market Street. Gradually two-horse buses were replaced by larger vehicles pulled by three horses. After 1878, horse-drawn trams made their appearance and crossed from one side of central Manchester to the other along Market Street, increasing its congestion. Then in 1901, the first electric trams appeared, adding to the variety of traffic. According to surveys undertaken in the early 20th century, thousands of people entered central Manchester every working day, many using Corporation Street from Victoria and Exchange Stations to reach the business and financial heart of the city around King Street. There was even a suggestion around 1906 that

Market Street should be pedestrianised, but nothing happened until the 1980s. Eventually, the trams disappeared and were replaced by motor buses, but the whole area would suffer from traffic jams, through the week and on Saturdays, as people poured into the centre of Manchester on Saturday afternoon to do their shopping.

Over the decades, the nature of the shops changed. Department stores like Lewis's and Henry's made their appearance in the late 19th century and began to attract shoppers. A glance through the directories during the 1920s and 1930s illustrates that many of the shops that existed on Market Street were associated with both men's and women's clothing, together with several jewellers and tobacconists. Both Withy Grove and Shudehill appeared to have been the location for furriers and jewellers, as well as those selling radios and radio parts, tobacconists and some selling food, usually greengrocery. There were few shops selling groceries and greengrocery in central Manchester as there were not the people living there to patronise them.

The 20th century saw the gradual deterioration in the state of much of the property in the area, especially that behind the main streets. Much of it was past its 'sell-by date'; action was needed to refurbish and redevelop large parts of the area to bring central Manchester up to scratch for the 20th century. The life-span of many of the buildings was extended by the Second World War. Rebuilding and redevelopment became impossible, but as a result of the blitz, in parts of central Manchester it became essential, as large areas were destroyed or severely damaged: areas like the Market Place, Piccadilly and the site of Victoria Buildings. However, much of the area covered by this book escaped with minimal damage, but it was obvious after the war that something was needed to be done to improve the area and bring this part of central Manchester up to a modern standard.

Expectations had changed as a result of the war and it was now necessary to try to meet some of these. It was clear that the area bounded by Market Street, High Street, Shudehill, Withy

Left: Henry's new store in Market Street which cost £250,000 to build in 1923. The architect, Charles Swain, also designed many cinemas and Manchester City's Maine Road stadium. His career ended with bankruptcy in 1934.

Below: The present Mrs Sarah's Chop House on Cross Street and Sam's Chop House on Back Pool Fold have their origins in Cockpit Hill.

Grove and Corporation Street would have to be redeveloped, together with a small area between Market Street, Cross Street and New Market. The redevelopment of this latter site resulted in the loss of buildings of importance to the history of Manchester, such as the premises where both the 'Manchester Guardian' and 'Manchester Evening News' had been edited and where, until around 1916, the 'Manchester Courier' also had its offices. In the late 1950s, plans were prepared for the redevelopment of Piccadilly, where there had been extensive bomb damage. Now it was a matter of dealing with this area. It appeared to be a case of 'out with the old and in with the new'. Little regard was paid to what was there and whether it could be retained; it had to go.

Later, some regrets were expressed that the redevelopment had not been more selective in the case of the facades of buildings, and some historic sites disappeared under new development. No opportunity was given to investigate the

Opposite: Palace Square looking towards Calender Street and Frank's Cloth Warehouse in 1969. The linen manufacturing company later moved to Fountain Street

Below: New Cannon Street towards Market Street. The poster in the window on the left advertises an all-night coffee bar. Many of these places sprang up in Manchester in the early 1960s. Frank Hatton, chairman of the Education Committee, thought they provided an outlet for the 'interests and vitality' of young people. But by 1964 there were concerns about the safety of the buildings, as well as drug trafficking and other criminal behaviour at the venues. The following year the Manchester Corporation Act was introduced to ensure clubs were registered, and to fine or close down offending businesses.

Chethams Library Archives

Construction of the Arndale beginning on the cleared site by Corporation Street.

Willow Publishing

Market Street blocked as demolition proceeded and the Arndale tower was under construction, July 1975.

Chethams Library Archives

The Arndale under construction, Market Street, with the building housing the John Collier and Timpson shops still remaining.

archaeology of the area to try to increase our knowledge of its earlier history.

It should also be pointed out that it was not the only area to see redevelopment. By the time plans were announced for the Arndale Centre, work had already started at the corner of Market Street and Corporation Street with the building of the new premises for Marks and Spencer.

The massive Arndale Centre attracted criticism with its appearance, especially the colour of the cladding. However, it brought new shops into central Manchester and provided some much needed covered shopping facilities for Mancunians. It is worth noting that across the road from the new development, some of Market Street's 19th-century buildings survived to provide a link with the past. A similar situation was also to be found along parts of Withy Grove, Shudehill and High Street. Links with the 19th

century remained and even today (2019) can still be discovered by the observant pedestrian.

Much was to change later when the building suffered by an IRA bomb in 1996. This gave the opportunity to re-assess the whole development and make improvements to its appearance. These changes had been mostly completed by 2002 when the Commonwealth Games were held in the city. It has to be remembered that although the redevelopment of this part of central Manchester attracted criticism and disapproval, it was a necessity if the city were to continue to be a major force not only regionally, but also nationally.

It should also be remembered that every part of a city has its own history and makes its own contribution to that city's history. The area covered by the Arndale is no exception.

Chris E Makepeace

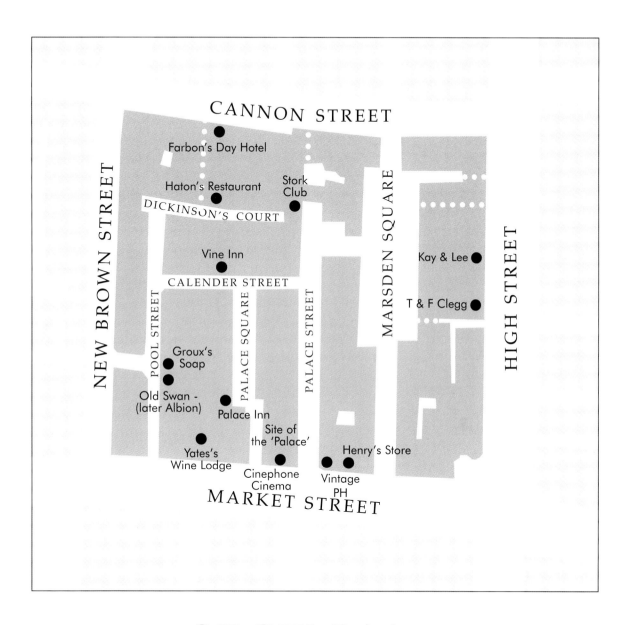

SECTION 1

Willow Publishing

Above, Market Street before the extension and modernisation
of Henry's store by 1962, on the left-hand side.

Opposite page, top: The corner of Market Street and High Street 1969.
Below: The BHS store 1969.

Keith Warrender

MARKET STREET

Keith Warrender

Right: Market Street 1969. S.E.T. referred to Selective Employment Tax which was introduced by the Wilson Government in 1966 to levy tax on employers who did not boost UK exports. It was replaced by VAT in 1973.

Below: Market Street in the 1950s. The open space next to Phillips' furnishing store had been caused by enemy bombing during WWII. The site was later temporarily used as a market.

Opposite page top: H Samuel had been trading at 97 Market Street since about 1880. It was named after Harriet Samuel who took over her father-in-law's clock-making business in Liverpool. In 1893 the company described itself as the largest manufacturer of watches in England. During that period they also had a branch at 1-3 Marsden Square.

Opposite page below: Various forms of transport on Market Street in the 1930s, looking towards the Royal Exchange. Note the Boots logo which has remained largely the same since it was introduced in the 1880s. The company opened a 'cash chemist' on Oldham Street in 1892 followed by branches at Market Street, Stretford Road and Downing Street by 1895.

Market Street c1950.

Willow Publish

24

Chris Makepeace

HENRY'S STORE

Henry Cohen had a small shop in London before coming to Manchester in 1891. He owned a shop at Travis Street off London Road and began Henry's in 1896. Further branches were started on Deansgate and around the North West, then in 1923 a new eight-storey department store was opened on Market Street. Their second department store in Birmingham was destroyed by bombing in WWII. In 1954 the company had 13 retail establishments, and by the early 1960s had modernised and extended the Market Street store. The new building trebled the retail space and doubled the frontage. It had the innovation of a curtain of heated air in the shop front.

Henry Cohen was one of the founders of Victoria Memorial Jewish Hospital. He was a major supporter of the 'Million Shillings Fund' for Manchester hospitals and active in local Jewish charities and institutions. His wife, Annie, came from the same village in Austria and claimed that

the births of their nine children always seemed to coincide with the opening of a new store. She took an active part in the company, buying for the haberdashery department and supervising sales. A fountain in Piccadilly Gardens was presented in memory of Henry Cohen and to commemorate the Coronation in 1953.

Four of Cohen's sons took over the running of Henry's. Leonard (1905-1971), chairman and joint managing director, was also a member of the Consumer Council. In addition to various roles within the Jewish community and Manchester Corporation, he was treasurer of Wythenshawe Labour Party and President of Manchester Literary and Philosophical Society. He was also a writer of Fabian pamphlets and a pioneer of the Civic Trust. After the £2.3 million takeover of Henry's by British Home Stores in 1968, he and his wife moved to Cyprus to pursue their interest in Greek history and literature.

THE 'PALACE'

The house at 44 Market Street was perhaps mockingly named 'The Palace' because royalty once stayed there. The 1740s Casson and Berry map includes a drawing of it, indicating it was one of Manchester's notable buildings. It stood back from Market Street, with a garden and a double flight of steps up to it. The map also revealed a private chapel within the grounds. Most of the street had half-timbered buildings, and this was one of the few brick-built properties.

It was the home of merchant John Dickenson who was Borough Reeve between 1749 and 1750, an important office in the manorial system. Close to the house on Market Street there was a pool where horses used to drink. Dickenson was a Jacobite sympathiser when Bonnie Prince Charlie (Charles Edward Stuart) came to Manchester with his army of 6000 troops, and he was accommodated at his residence.

The Prince arrived at about 2pm on Saturday 29th November 1745 at Dickenson's house. His supporters flocked to welcome him as he dined. Dickenson was also involved in the collection of pledges on the levy the prince had imposed on Manchester. The following day Charles inspected his troops and on the Monday, left to march south in his unsuccessful bid for the throne.

By that time Dickenson had just purchased the Birch Hall estate, and the residence on Market Street would have been his town house. It became the home of James Borron, a fustian manufacturer, and descendent of the Dickensons. After his death in 1804 it was turned into the Palace Inn and remained open until 1837. A post coach service to Liverpool and Leeds began from here in 1807.

Before the inn's demolition it was used first as a committee room by Lord Egerton and Bootle Wilbraham during their election as representatives for the southern division, and also for an anti-poor law convention of 300 delegates from Yorkshire, Cheshire and Lancashire. The Bee Coffee and Dining Rooms below the inn had remained open. It was claimed that this was the first substantial restaurant in Manchester. Both this and the inn remained under Dickenson family ownership at the time of the Market Street improvements in the 1820s.

Some items were saved from Dickenson's house and removed to Birch Hall, including the stone pillars at the entrance to his house, the bed on which the Prince slept, a pair of pistols left by the Prince and his pocket handkerchief. The family had cut up a blanket used by the Prince and distributed it to friends. In 1838 the historic building was demolished and replaced by a new inn, shops and warehouses on the site.

Benjamin Binyon became the proprietor of the new Palace Inn and Coffee House at 2 Palace Square on 15 October 1838. He announced it had been designed for the 'hasty traveller or passing stranger' and that tea and coffee could be ordered throughout the day and be 'supplied in five seconds'. He had previously been a wine seller at 101 Market Street on the corner of High Street.

But three months later, due to Binyon's bankruptcy, it was auctioned. In 1844 it re-opened as the Palace Inn Steak Chop and Coffee House, then about 1860 it was renamed the Crystal Palace. It was purchased in 1894 by Peter Yates and, along with the Old Swan, later became the new Albion Hotel.

PALACE BUILDINGS

Another reference to the 1745 visit of Charles Stuart can be seen in the 1849 OS map which indicates the Palace Buildings bounded by Palace Street and Marsden Place. They were demolished in 1881 and were the last to be re-built on the new building line to complete the widening of Market Street. The name of Palace Buildings (the last building on the right of the photograph - Samuel Burman's) referred more appropriately to the block at 93 Market Street enclosed by Palace Square and Palace Street which was effectively the site of the old Palace Inn. In 1905 the building was demolished and work began on a new building. It was completed in 1906 with Provincial Cinematograph Theatres Ltd securing the lease on the property on 22 March 1910.

Trouble at the Vintage

The Vintage Pub was at 2 Palace Street and 99 Market Street in 1896 selling wines, spirits and ales. In 1908 the licensee, Henry Ward, was fined twenty shillings and £6 costs for allowing 'loose women' on his premises. His mother managed the pub which was entered down a flight of steps. Police witnesses said that women known to them as 'Radcliffe Katie', 'Cabby' and 'Sheffield Emily' had been seen in there. The women were mostly well-dressed unlike the Angel Meadow women who were seen here or at Deansgate. Ward and his mother were in trouble again in 1908 after being caught selling bottled and draught Bass which was not made by the brewers. The next year the renewal of the licence was refused because the pub had harboured disorderly characters.

BILL BENNY'S STORK CLUB

In the early 1950s, regulations were eased in the registration of clubs and an estimated 1000 new clubs opened nationally between 1954 and 1958. The Stork Club was at the end of Palace Street in the basement of number 19. It was one of Manchester's earliest nightclubs and open by 1955, when it was advertising for cabaret acts of ten-minute duration. It was run by Bill Benny, known by many as the heavyweight 'Man Mountain' in his other role as professional wrestler.

His wrestling career began in his teens and he became a favourite with fans because of his villainous activities in the ring. He would goad crowds into a frenzy and they enjoyed seeing him thrown out of the ring or disqualified for persistent fouling. In a bout at Hartlepool, he broke the ring ropes, pulled up the floor of the ring and bent and twisted the steel supports. In another contest, after losing the fight, he chased his opponent out of the ring all the way to the dressing room. However, in a later fight, after perhaps accidentally knocking out the other wrestler, he carried him to the dressing room.

Benny had red hair and beard and has been described as 'a lisping, hare-lipped Henry VIII look-alike'. During the making of the 'Mutiny on the Bounty' film he was a stand-in for the actor Charles Lawton. He also played a wrestler in the 1950 musical comedy film High Jinks in Society.

He was born in Brighton in 1918, real name Stanley B Benjamin. His father, Jack, was a Jewish immigrant from Russia. By 1939 Benny worked at the family grocers and fishmongers in London and was known as Billy Benjamin. He first appeared as 'Big Bill Benny' in 1944. In the ring he was well-known around the country, and fought fellow villains such as Jack Pye at the King's Hall, Belle Vue. Another wrestler claimed that Benny used to travel free to his bouts.

Benny was said to board trains dressed as a railway guard, carrying a lamp, to avoid paying the fare. He also had another ring persona as The Vampire, donning a black mask.

Benny reduced his wrestling appearances to become a nightclub pioneer, with business partners band-leader Vic Lewis and Dougie Wood, bringing top performers from the USA including Ella Fitzgerald, The Platters and Judy Garland. With Jack McCall, Benny opened further venues: the Northern, Devonshire and Levenshulme Sporting Clubs and the Cabaret Club. Roy Castle and Tessie O'Shea were among the artists who appeared at his clubs. In 1960 Benny also bought the Hulme Hippodrome for £35,000 to stage variety and striptease shows. It was later changed it into a bingo hall. Benny and Lewis also put on shows in London starring the Ted Heath Band and Johnny Mathis.

Benny became well-known around Manchester. He promoted wrestling at the Free Trade Hall, and appeared in the film 'Hell Is a City' which was centred around Manchester. He featured in an early scene at the Lacy Arms pub (the Fatted Calf, Cromford Court) and in the gambling sequence on the Oldham moor where he had a few lines. Benny was in the film's promotion stills with Stanley Baker, and possibly advised on the fight scenes. He had a fleet of cars bearing the number plates BB1, BB2 and BB3.

In September 1963, aged 45, he collapsed and died suddenly of a heart attack at his Rusholme flat. Ironically, on the day of his death, he learned that two people with connections to his clubs had been involved in car crashes and decided it was safer to walk home from work! In the Stage newspaper obituary, it described him as 'The King of Clubs' who had introduced the best cabaret entertainment outside London.

The film 'Sex From a Stranger' showing at the Cinephone in March 1969, was described by the Guardian newspaper as a 'pretentious French farrago'(hotpotch).

THE CINEPHONE

The cinema opened on Tuesday 29th August 1910 at the Palace Buildings, 93 Market Street. This was the City's first cinema with its own permanent site, although it was not purpose-built. There was seating for 800 and the takings from the opening night showing were donated to Ancoats Hospital. The Era newspaper described the interior of the cinema as 'luxurious and perfectly equipped' and with good fire precautions. The previous year had seen the passing of the Cinematograph Act which stipulated that highly inflammable film stock had to be projected from fire-proof booths. This effectively ended the many temporary film shows around the country.

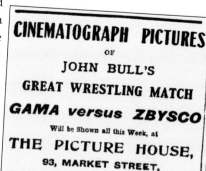

CINEMATOGRAPH PICTURES
OF
JOHN BULL'S
GREAT WRESTLING MATCH
GAMA versus ZBYSCO
Will be Shown all this Week, at
THE PICTURE HOUSE,
93, MARKET STREET.
Open till 10-30.   Admission 6d. and 1s.

following December, the company opened the first purpose-built cinema in Manchester, on Oxford Street. By 12 September the Market Street Picture House was showing the film of a wrestling match between 'Gama' and 'Zbysco'. It was open daily until 10.30pm and admission was 6d, balcony 1s, children half price. The Head Master of Eton questioned whether it was good for children to attend such places, but the proprietors of the cinema company argued that it was an opportunity to develop children's imaginations. Films included selections from operas.

In May 1910 the company issued 40,000 shares to raise £100,000 capital, in order to finance the

The cinema was known as The Picture House, and was owned by the newly-formed Provincial Cinematograph Theatres Ltd. The lease for the building had been signed on 22nd March 1910 with Harold, Reginald and George Cohen. The

opening of fourteen new theatres. They had opened a cinema in Dublin and were planning to introduce further cinematograph theatres in Birmingham, Leeds, Glasgow, Edinburgh and Belfast. All the sites were in busy shopping areas.

An indication of the picture house's growing popularity was reflected by the fine imposed by the authorities in 1912 for not keeping the cinema's passageways clear. A build-up had been caused by 250 people gathering in the lounge and a further 225 standing in the aisles waiting for vacant seats. A music licence was granted to both the Market Street and Oxford Street cinemas so that orchestras could accompany the silent films. By 1913, an estimated eight million people visited the cinematograph theatres nationally

Musee of Mirth

Before the opening of the Market Street Picture House, the premises had links with various forms of moving pictures. The Manchester and Salford Mutoscope Company was listed there in 1900 but within two years had gone into liquidation. The mutoscope peep-show flicker-card machine had been introduced in 1895.

By 1908 the basement at Market Street had become the 'Musee of Mirth' with half-hour shows for two pence and machines giving palm readings. There were no seats, and the audience were on a sloping floor. It meant that customers had to lean on the person in front to keep their balance. Unsurprisingly this was not a popular venue!

each week. DW Griffith's epic 'Birth of a Nation' was shown at the Market Street Theatre in 1915, two days before it opened in London.

The Market Street and Oxford Street picture houses were purchased in 1925 by a private partnership of James Emery, an Alderman and Mayor of Salford, and Enrique Carreras of the Manchester Theatre Royal and Veno Trust. 'The Talk of Hollywood' was the first sound picture to be shown here in 1930.

As audiences dropped, it re-opened in September 1949, after a month's closure, as a news theatre owned by Jacey Cinemas, showing travelogues, cartoons and newsreels. It became the Continental Cinema in 1950 screening the best European films, but due to low demand resumed as a news theatre in 1952. It was renamed the Cinephone in 1955 to show the best of world cinema. While it did occasionally show quality films, it became better known for films such as 'Seduced in Sodom' and 'I am Sexy'. The cinema closed on 14 January 1974 after six decades, due to the Arndale Development. The films shown in the farewell programme were 'The Queer - the Erotic' and 'Where Are You Going All Naked?'. Other cinemas which closed that year included the Gaumont on Oxford Street and the ABCs at Eccles, Sale and Wythenshawe. After the Cinephone was demolished, a projector was found crushed in the debris.

Keith Warrender

The demolition of the old Palace buildings (right) in 1905. Note the sign
for Yates's Wine Lodge which was along Palace Square to the left.

OLD SWAN

The Old Swan was situated at 3 Pool Street. In 1776 Alice Rowcroft of Pool Street was fined for allowing her pigs to run loose in a public area. George Hill had a public house here by 1842 and was attracting customers with a painting of the racehorse Beeswing, one of the greatest thoroughbreds of the sport, winning 51 of her races out of 63, including the Ascot Gold Cup in 1842.

A meeting was held at the Old Swan in 1843 by the committee campaigning for the release of Richard Oastler of Huddersfield. He is credited with being one of the first to protest against children's long working hours. Oastler had got into financial difficulties and was imprisoned in 1840 but was released in 1846 after supporters paid off his £3,200 debt. The fight for change resulted in the 1847 Factory Act, otherwise known as the Ten Hours Act, which meant that women and children could work for no more than ten hours a day. It took further Acts in 1850 and 1853 to remedy some of the defects in the 1847 Parliamentary Act. Underhand methods were used against the campaigners. A letter opposing the change in hours was sent in 1846 to the Manchester Guardian purporting to be from James Hobson, an operative from King Street, Stockport. Further investigation found that no-one of that name lived in any of Stockport's three King Streets! Business owners retained their profits by making employees work in shifts and by increasing men's hours up to 16 a day. Until then, for young people, their lives had just been bed and work. With the new leisure time, football and cricket became popular. The 1847 Act was one of a series to obtain factory reform, but it was to take until 1901 even to raise the minimum working age to 12.

Pool Street from Swan Lane.

Manchester licensed victuallers met at the Old Swan in 1844 over concerns that they would have to pay window tax, even though shopkeepers were exempt. They agreed to send a national petition to the government. Window tax had been introduced in the 17th century and was repealed in 1851 to be replaced by a buildings tax.

John Sloan, comedian and previously manager of the Theatre Royal, took over the Old Swan in 1847. He made his first appearance on the stage in 1842 at the Drury Lane Theatre. In 1846 he converted the Riding School on Lower Mosley Street, Manchester, into the Royal Promenade Concert Hall which was very successful. Sloan held gentlemen-only nightly concerts in the upstairs concert room of the Old Swan during 1847. They ceased later in the year after the inn was damaged by the great fire, with all the furniture and stock destroyed. Sloan was then also lessee of the Queen's Theatre. He later went to America where he performed and managed theatres, and died in Liverpool in 1861.

In 1926, the Old Swan, along with the Palace Hotel, became known as the New Albion Hotel. Previously the Albion had been in Piccadilly for many years and was one of the city's finest old hotels. In 1906 a meeting was held at the Piccadilly premises to form the National Union of Journalists, with members from around the North West. The Piccadilly site became the Woolworth's store. The new Albion Hotel, off Market Street, bought by Peter Yates for £25,000, had 40 bed-rooms, and an oak-panelled dining room.

The 75-bedroomed Albion Hotel at its previous site in Piccadilly, purchased by Peter Yates in 1901.

Pool Street off Market Street.

Above: 1872 advertisement. Around 1910 the hotel claimed it provided the best 5-course lunch in town, with 'real turtle always ready, 1s per plate'.

Billy Connor behind the bar in the Albion smoke room. There was great sadness amongst customers when it had to close for the coming Arndale development.

Staff meal at the closure of the Old Bank Grill on 87 Market Street in April 1971. This was also owned by Yates's and was a teetotal establishment.

In the Yates Brothers' history of the company in 1984, the Albion Hotel was described as 'warm and cosy and welcoming, even though it was poky and of poor layout. Everywhere the floor boards creaked and one had the feeling that the whole thing was one tremendous fire risk. The food was good, the service always with a smile and one remembers the manageress Miss Thiede, Tom Connor (cloak attendant), Billy Connor, his brother, in the smoke room bar, and John McKernan the head waiter'. The walls were covered in Bateman drawings such as 'The Guest Who Passed the Port the Wrong Way'. First-time visitors were surprised when the after-dinner coffee was served in cups with no handles. This was because Peter Yates believed that coffee should not be drunk too hot but allowed to cool in order not to burn the stomach. Therefore it was reasoned that if cups were too hot to handle then the contents were too hot to drink.

The Albion Hotel and Yates's Wine Lodge, Market Street.

YATES'S WINE LODGE

Yates's Wine Lodge moved to 2 Palace Square and 91a Market Street in 1895 from 133-5 Market Street opposite Lewis's. They had another lodge on Oldham Street. Peter Yates and his brother Simon established the wine lodges in 1884.

The first was at the Angel Hotel in Oldham which they bought from their aunt, Mary Addison, who greatly influenced their business values and practices. They quickly expanded that year to Manchester, Preston and London, and within twenty years they had twenty lodges. It began in 1880 with a small corner shop in Preston selling large glasses of sherry, then later cream gin. In 1884 they rented premises on Market Street in Manchester.

By 1904 Yates Brothers and Company had several other premises in Manchester: the Rowland Hill

"WILO"

Hotel Oldham Street, a warehouse Cheetham Street, the Waverley Hotel 14-16 Oldham Street, the Crystal Palace Hotel 2 Palace Street, a shop 88 Tib Street, a warehouse and offices Carnarvon Street - which later became the head office, the Albion Hotel Piccadilly, the Grapes Hotel Oldham Street and the Reindeer Hotel Market Street.

Yates wanted his wine lodges to be places where a working man could take his wife for an evening out to enjoy good food and wines. He tried to serve quality products at reasonable prices. His motto throughout his life was 'Moderation is true temperance'.

Peter Yates had a house in Fleetwood and owned the first private car licensed in the Fylde area. He travelled around Spain and Portugal buying wines for the business until the outbreak of WWII.

He rarely drank and encouraged moderation in alcohol consumption. Staff were under orders not to serve anyone who displayed the slightest trace of drunkenness. In the afternoons, after closing time, the lodges sold bowls of soup and tea. The company also established teetotal taverns in Manchester and Blackpool where people used to queue on cold days for penny bowls of soup.

Yates regarded himself as a reformer of pubs by providing meals to attract family trade. Yates's had their own beef farms, laundry, bakery, and flour mill to produce unbleached flour. They served only wholemeal bread at the pubs, and sold their flour with the slogan 'The whiter the bread, the sooner you're dead'. Yates's also had their own brand of tea, sold three sorts of sardines and had cigars imported from Cuba because Yates preferred them to cigarettes. There was a 'display window' at Palace Street where people watched women making cigars.

Peter Yates used to tour the lodges not only to keep an eye on the business but also to share his views on healthy living, which included sleeping in the prone position and reducing car speed limits. He was quite short and used to stand on a specially-made platform to give his talk. Usually twice-yearly he issued a publication entitled 'Common Sense' which offered advice on health matters. He recommended Wrexham lager beer (in which he had no financial interest) as a wholesome liquid food for the seriously ill. He advised rheumatism sufferers to sit rather than stand, and lie rather than sit to take strain off the heart. He warned that roast potatoes were almost indigestible because they were impregnated with fats. Yates was also a vigorous campaigner for the interests of the wine trade.

Peter Yates' interests outside business were numerous. He was a keen golfer, on the council of the Royal Lancashire Agricultural Society, a member of Fleetwood Literary Society and several sports clubs. After his death in 1944, the company celebrated his birthday with the

annual issue of Founder's Day port for customers to drink a toast to him. The company continued to be run by the Yates family. Yates's were the first to import Australian wine and were well-known for their 'blobs', a mixture of white wine, sugar, lemon and hot water. They were also the country's biggest importers of port. The Market Street Wine Lodge property was bought by Arndale Developments in 1968.

The flour mill at 93 Spear Street, behind the Grapes Hotel on Oldham Street.

Peter Yates

Keith Worrender

Back street ticket sales.

Bobby McDermott
'King of the barrowboys'

McDermott earned the nickname because he not only owned many sites in the city but also supported the rights of street traders. He was the son of a fruit-seller and in 1939 was an apprentice furniture upholsterer. He did not drink or smoke, wore a ring on every finger and was said to be a clever 'wheeler dealer'. McDermott could supply tickets for all major sporting events and was on first-name terms with footballers, judges, councillors and hardened criminals. He owned a warehouse on New Cannon Street which was also the venue of the Card gambling club. During the filming of 'Hell Is a City' he advised Stanley Baker on the criminal underworld in Manchester, and spent time with the film star at the Cromford Club. After a ban of over twenty years, barrow boys were officially allowed back in the city centre in 1971 on 17 sites. When McDermott died in 1980, the traders were joined by over 200 mourners from around the country.

Keith Worrender

Seller on the corner of Market Street and Pool Street.

Keith Worrender

Keith Worrender

Above and top: Barrows loaded and stored in the back streets off Market Street.

Keith Warrender

Storage area for barrows behind Market Street.

Royal soap-maker

Groux's Improved Soap was being advertised at 6 Pool Street in 1855. Louis Groux from Hamburg had been producing soap in London since the early 1840s. He advertised his 'toilet and fancy soaps' as being superior to any other. He claimed they kept linen whiter, could be used by the Navy to use with salt water, and that they retained their weight, shape and perfume. He was helped by the abolition of soap tax by William Gladstone's government in 1853.

From 1855 he advertised his products as being used by Queen Victoria and the Royal family as well as in the Royal laundry. After his company closed in 1857, he partnered with James Crossley in Manchester until 1859. Then by 1862 he joined with Hibbard and Ryan in Sheffield, where he patented improvements in machinery and soap manufacture. After the partnership was dissolved in 1863 he went to New York where he continued in soap making until his death about 1878.

Market Street.

Market Street.

The great fire of 1847

On 11th August 1847 one of Manchester's worst fires occurred. The huge fire burnt through the area of Market Street, New Brown Street and Pool Street. It was thought to have begun about 7.45pm in the upstairs premises of Frederick Smith, manufacturers and suppliers of fine paper for booksellers and stationers, in New Brown Street. It was probably started by a fire used to heat glue not being properly doused at the end of the day. It was a windy summer's evening and the blaze quickly spread through the whole of the four-storey block, with nearby properties in Calender Street catching fire. At its height, the flames could be seen ten miles away in Bowdon. It was thought that the entrance to the block on New Brown Street and the square service well in the centre of the warehouse acted as a flue for the fire.

The messenger who had been sent to the Police yard to report the fire was completely out of breath after running so quickly and could not speak, but luckily a second messenger arrived to pass on the details. The yard was on the site of the present Town Hall. The command went out from Thomas Rose, the fire brigade superintendent, to send all the town's fire engines. The Salford brigade also assisted, and the Stockport and Bolton brigades were alerted but later turned back. There were fears that the fire would spread to Cannon Street and High Street but the fire-fighters did well to contain it within a relatively small area.

Samuel Brooks was working at his bank on Market Street when the fire started. Realising the seriousness of the situation, he quickly arranged for all available omnibuses to take vital documents from the bank to a nearby location where they were guarded through the night.

Cunliffe and Brooks' bank building was partially destroyed, but he opened for business the following morning in King Street.

Some of the businesses managed to bring out goods and property from the premises as the fire raged. More might have been saved if the fire had occurred during business hours. Big crowds watched the proceedings and helped where they were able but it was reported that looting also took place. At ten o'clock the fire was under control and by midnight it was thought that

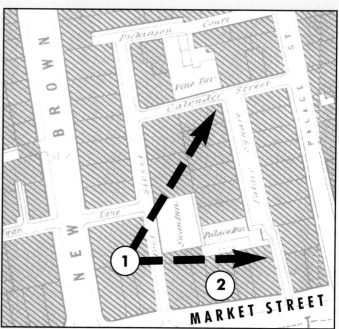

Extent of the fire:
1. The warehouse block containing Frederick Smith, booksellers and stationers, where the fire originated.
2. Cunliffe Brooks' Bank, Market Street.

it had been put out, but at 2am another fire broke out in a nearby warehouse which had to be dealt with. The Old Swan Inn on Pool Street was amongst the buildings damaged. Fortunately no-one was injured during the incident. Rose, the fire superintendent who kept a record of all the fires he attended, calculated it had caused over £41,000 of damage.

DICKINSON'S COURT

Dickinson's Court is shown on Laurent's 1794 map but not named. It was not listed in the 1800 directory but in the 1814 Manchester Mercury there is a reference to Thomas Tallent, of Dickinson's Court. Tallent was a merchant in haberdashery and drapery and had a warehouse on Cannon Street in 1805. His great-grandson, Charles Tallent Bateman (1852-1927), was a solicitor and had many interests in the city.

He was one of the founder members of the Lancashire and Cheshire Antiquarian Society, and wrote extensively about Manchester's history. He was also involved in the formation of the Peak District and Northern Counties Footpaths Preservation Society and prominent in helping to secure a right of way along the Snake footpath beneath the slopes of Kinder Scout. Parkinson's Britannia Chop-House was situated at Dickinson's Court in 1853. It was taken over in 1856 by Joseph Haton who later applied for a licence. In his application, he said that the eating and beerhouse was popular with clerks and warehouse workers. In 1881 it became known as Haton's Dining Rooms. By 1911 it had become the Anchor Inn. The licensee claimed that the Anchor was the oldest in Manchester, but seemed to be referring to an inn of that name which was listed on Market Street Lane in 1772. At that time it was partly a beerhouse and restaurant. Although the authorities recommended it should close in 1911, it remained open until 1920.

Vine Tavern fire, Calender Street

The Vine Tavern, which could be accessed either in Calender Street or Palace Street, was in existence by 1840 with George Massey the publican. That same year Alfred Barlow took over. It was to prove a difficult period for him.

The pub was damaged by a fire in March which destroyed the two adjoining warehouses. Barlow had been awakened at 5am by the sound of something falling. At first he thought it was criminals trying to break open his window shutters as they had done before. Then he heard the sound of breaking glass at the back, looked out of a window and saw smoke coming out of the warehouse next door.

He raised the alarm then got his household out of the premises. The back of the tavern caught fire but he was able to remove most of his furniture and other goods.

The fire fighters had problems with 'plugs', the access points to the water-mains, not working and also shortages of personnel. Mr Rose the Fire Superintendent had to pay bystanders to help with the fire engines. The fire was thought to have started in a four-storey warehouse next to the Vine and may have begun the previous evening when people noticed the smell of fire. The fire was under control within two hours. Two safes were recovered from the ruined warehouses with their contents slightly singed but intact. Firemen spent the rest of the day retrieving as much as they could from the damaged warehouses. No fire-fighters were injured but two horses in one of the warehouses died in the fire. But for Alfred Barlow, there was a much greater tragedy, when his wife Eleanor, age 31, died a few months later. In 1860 there was a meeting here to establish the Second Vine Building Society. The tavern had been demolished by 1870.

Farbon's Day Hotel

The hotel was opened in 1875 by Robert Farbon. It had cost over £2,000 to improve and extend the premises at 58-60 Cannon Street. At the age of eighteen, he had been a compositor in Leighton Buzzard, but in 1859 he was insolvent after a failed printing business in Manchester. By 1868 he owned eating houses in Tib Street and then Thomas Street. The same year he had been ordered by the court at Horncastle to pay 2s 6d weekly to a mother for fathering her child.

There were fires at Farbon's hotel about 1875 and in 1880 when the floorboards directly under the cooking range caught fire. Farbon wanted to retire in 1880 and put the hotel up for sale.

It was described as having 12 bedrooms, a billiard room with three championship tables, and 1000 customers daily.

There were no buyers, and the hotel continued until 1883 when Farbon's business went into liquidation. It re-opened briefly as a vegetarian restaurant and later as Brown's Restaurant. The property was re-built, and by 1886 the building was for sale as a warehouse.

Farbon, however, had began a new venture about 1885. His 'Trading Company of England', was producing 'Farbon's Army and Navy Sauce' a product made with fruits and spices which was available nationally until 1887. Farbon died in 1892 and his wife, Elizabeth, went on to be landlady of the Commercial Inn, Prestwich where she was fined in 1894 for selling alcohol after licensing hours.

MARSDEN SQUARE

The square was named after James Marsden who owned the ornate three-storey house on Market Street Lane close to John Dickenson's home, and shown on Casson and Berry's maps in the 1740s. The building, enclosed by railings, stood back from the street and was approached by steps. It had a coat of arms over the front door and a cupola and four stone figures on the roof. Before its development as a square, the land had been used for brick-making. Part of the land was covered by a pool which was used in brick production. Marsden was a Jacobite sympathiser and Lord George Murray, the Duke of Atholl, was billeted at his house during Charles Stuart's stay in Manchester in 1745. Marsden was a wealthy man with other streets and courts named after him.

Marsden (or Marsden's) Square, along with Cannon Street and St Ann's Square, was once regarded as the best and most genteel part of the town. By 1772 it had become industrialised with fustian, silk, linen and woollen manufacturers situated here. There used to be posts at the Cannon Street end of the square restricting access, which were removed in 1822. The first library belonging to the Manchester Law Society was sited in Marsden

Mr Marsden's imposing house.

Square in 1823. By 1838 it had 700 books, and later moved to Kennedy Street.

MURDER

In 1826 there was a murder in the square which shocked the people of Manchester. Thomas Price, a fustian merchant, was found dead in his premises above the savings bank. About 2pm, witnesses noticed smoke coming from the building and the fire brigade forced their way into the warehouse. They found Price's partly-burnt body with severe head injuries. Smoke was coming from smouldering pieces of fustian by his body, and it seemed the murderer had started the fire. Mr Price had been regarded as an exemplary character with a wife and six children. Later a concealed pistol was discovered in the room where Price had been murdered.

James Evans, Price's warehouseman, was suspected of the murder. He was said to have an 'unhappy violence of temper' and arrested. However he was acquitted through lack of evidence at the Lancaster Assizes and the murderer was never discovered.

COUNTY FORUM

The County Forum dining rooms at 2 Marsden Square were advertised in 1883 when Dr Richard Pankhurst gave a speech there during his campaign to be a Manchester MP. He was not successful nor in a second attempt at Rotherhithe two years later. His views in support of Irish Home Rule and secular education did not make him widely popular. Emmeline, his wife, was the leader of the British Suffragette movement. He became known as the 'Red Doctor' after helping to establish the Independent Labour Party with Emmeline.

The Manchester County Forum dining rooms moved the following year to 103 Market Street and then in 1892 to 50A Market Street. An advertisement at that time claimed they were cheaper and quicker than other restaurants in the city. In the 1890s, debates with businessmen and farmers took place on Tuesday and Friday afternoons, and for working-class men on Saturday and Sunday evenings. The catering and hotel business had been run as a separate company until 1904 when it went into liquidation

Marsden Square from Cannon Street c1900.

and the premises auctioned. The public debates continued and by 1906 the Forum was meeting at 5 Cromford Court. The Forum was regarded as an important debating institution where lively discussion took place, often led by prominent political figures. They included James Connolly, an Irish rebel who was executed during the last war.

A Manchester evening paper in 1939 claimed that the debating society, which jealously guarded the rights of free speech, had been founded in 1812. The Society operated under strict rules enforced by the chairman. The opening speaker was allowed thirty minutes to present the case, then subsequent contributors were given ten minutes each. The 1939/40 programme of debates included: 'Russia and Democracy', 'The Influence of Religion in Germany', and 'Should the Lay Magistracy be Abolished?'

In 1940, meetings were briefly held in the banqueting hall of the Victoria Hotel, after the outbreak of WWII. The Sunday meetings resumed in 1947 at the Mitre Hotel with the Lord Mayor adding his support. The organisation hoped to educate young people in public speaking and current affairs. By 1956 the Forum met at 41 Hilton Street and two years later, Leslie Lever MP was outlining his views on Middle East issues at the Forum.

INSPIRATION FOR DICKENS

The square, described in 1951 as a 'Georgian backwater' with its fine old doorways was thought to have been the inspiration for a London street in Charles Dickens' 'Nicholas Nickleby' novel. (See also Cheeryble House, Cannon Street). In the 1960s there were two basement coffee bars in the square at the rear of the British Home Stores; Drake's Drum and Hatchway.

The 'nearly' square

Marsden Square could be called 'the nearly square' because it was under consideration for a number of significant projects due to its central position, but none of the schemes came to fruition. In 1845 it was debated whether the Exchange should be re-housed there with part of the square covered with a glass roof to create a trading area. After much consideration the Exchange was extended on its existing site. In 1858 it was strongly advocated as the site for the new General Post Office, but Brown Street was eventually selected. The square was one of a number of possible locations in 1899 for lunch-hour city centre outdoor concerts, and in 1914 it was discussed as a tram terminus.

Keith We

Marsden Square, towards the rear of British Home Stores and Tino Café 1969.

Keith Warrender

Second-hand record shop, 21 Marsden Square.

Ross Collection

Marsden Square. Note the ornate doorway on the right slightly obscured by the flue.

Keith Warrender

Corner of High Street and Market Street.

HIGH STREET

In 1650 the High Street area was open fields but by the 1760s it had become a residential area with houses on either side, stretching from Market Street Lane to Turner Street. Thomas Johnson's house (See page 168) is indicated about where Cannon Street would later join High Street. Some of the wealthier people lived there with most having back gardens. Thirty years later by the time of Laurent's 1793 map, all of the gardens and open land of the 'Lost District' had gone, with many new streets and courts between Market Street Lane and Cannon Street. By then, High Street was changing from a residential area into a place of commerce.

Casson's and Berry's 1746 map shows the High Street and Marsden Square residential areas with many householders having back gardens. Beyond are gardens and fields stretching to Shudehill. Note the figure 34 (circled) which indicates the site of Mr Dickenson's private chapel within the grounds of his house which was later named 'The Palace'.

By the time of the 1861 Census, the only resident in Marsden Square was a watchman for the warehouses.

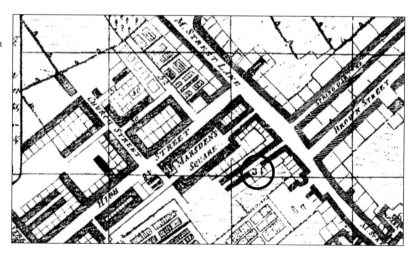

Keith Warrender

clurers fashion shop

TWENTY THOUSAND WOMEN CAN'T BE WRONG

This season about 20,000 women have bought coats and dresses direct from us at factory price. So far as we know everyone was more than satisfied and many went out of their way to say so. We send lots of coats abroad also. U.S.A., Canada, South Africa, Australia. One woman in U.S.A. even started a business selling our coats to her friends.

Come and buy at factory price at the factory showroom 15B High Street, only a few yards from Market Street— the best coat and dress value in all England.

Illustrated is a shirt-waist dress in Ferguson's cotton, which needs little or no ironing. It has deep pockets on the bodice and the sleeves are gathered on the cuffs to match the skirt. Cut, make, and finish are better than most and second to none. An amazing bargain at £2.5.0. In Powder Blue, Pink, and Turquoise.

Fine coats in pure wool cloths that are wonderful value by any standard. Pure wool velours £6.10.0. Fine Tweeds and all the latest wool cloths and every coat at factory price.

T. & F. CLEGG LTD.
COAT AND DRESS MANUFACTURERS

Fashion at Factory Price

" An outstanding weakness in our economy is that increased efficiency in manufacturing industry has not been matched by comparable improvements in distribution. The benefits of cost reductions in the factories have not been reaching the customer."—"Manchester Guardian," May 16th, 1958.

We have brought down the cost of distribution by doing it ourselves. The savings are immense and you save pounds. Hundreds of good quality coats and dresses straight out of our Manchester factory, and straight into our own shops. Ample space, private fitting rooms and no sales talk. Entire satisfaction or money back without fuss always. We believe this to be the best coat and dress value in England.

The coat illustrated is in a selection of 18-ounce all-wool tweeds, 36 to 42 hips, £6.10.0. Hips 44 at £6.17.6. Fine coats in Yorkshire Tweeds and pure wool velours, £6.10.0. Handwoven Shetland Tweed coats, £7.7.6. Our famous Handwoven Harris Tweed coats, £8.5.0. New Spring dresses in Ferguson's cottons mainly £2.9.6. Sheath dresses in Stevensons' plain lightweight suiting, £2.2.6.

Today our new shop opens at 65 Hanover Street, Liverpool, a few yards from Church Street and Bold Street, the next building to Cranes, next but one to shops on the corner of Church Street. 100 yards from Liverpool Central Station. There is also a shop in the centre of Manchester at 15B High Street. The addresses of our shops given below.

CLEGGS COAT AND DRESS MANUFACTURERS
15B HIGH STREET, MANCHESTER 1
9 yards from Market St. Open 9 to 5-30 every day incl. Weds. and Sats.
65 HANOVER STREET, LIVERPOOL
9 to 5-30 p.m., Monday to Saturday. Closed Wednesdays 12-30 p.m.
PRINCES STREET, STOCKPORT. 241 STAMFORD STREET, ASHTON.
VICTORIA SQUARE, BOLTON. 3 NEWTON STREET, HYDE.
Brownsfield Mill, 104 Gt. Ancoats Street, Manchester 4.

1959

T & F Clegg Ltd, 15b High St

In 1946 Cleggs Ltd were based at Newton Street, Hyde, but by 1959 they had moved to the Brownsfield Mill, Great Ancoats Street and had stores in Manchester, Stockport, Bolton, Ashton, Hyde and Liverpool, and were looking to expand into Yorkshire, Lancashire and the Potteries. In 1967 they were listed at Royal Mill, Redhill Street, Manchester along with eight shops and 150 employees.

Willow Publishing

Kay and Lee

Lee Family History

William Lee

Kay and Lee, at 17 High Street, were manufacturers and wholesalers of men's and boys' clothing. William Lee (1847-1904) co-founded the firm in 1873 with John Kay at Watling Street. After Kay's death in 1878, Lee continued to run the company which had moved to High Street by 1890. They also had premises at Allum Street, Ancoats. In 1881 the firm employed nearly 400 people. The firm donated 120 overcoats and 70 pairs of trousers in 1897 for the Lord Mayor's appeal to help the distressed in Ireland. Then in 1902 they gave 41 suits to destitute children as part of a city initiative. The clothing was stamped on the inside to prevent it being sold on or pawned.

In 1955 the company patented the self-supporting waistband for boys' and men's clothing, under the brand name of 'Gripu'. Lee, at his death, left today's equivalent of almost £7.5 million, some of which he left to various local hospitals and orphanages. The company was taken over in 1957 by Boardman, Marden Ltd, clothing manufacturers from Stockport. Between the late 1960s and 1990s Kay and Lee were situated at 27-29 Church Street.

(Left) The Pico coffee bar, one of six Pico cafés in the centre of Manchester in the 1970s. (Centre) Marsden Place and (right) the Florin Snack Bar 17a, High Street. Compare the building with the illustration on the opposite page and note that the top two storeys had been removed.

Rose Brothers' handbags and Derber's Anglo-Italian footwear, 19 High Street.

SECTION 2

SWAN COURT

The Higher Swan

The inn on Swan Court was originally the Saracen's Head licensed house, to which was added the Higher Swan coaching inn. The property extended to the gardens of Marsden Square. In April 1753 an ostler was found hanging in the stables. The inquest brought a verdict of suicide which then was regarded as a crime. As was the practice in those times, the body was dragged on a sledge and buried at Four Lane Ends. This would have been a place on the outskirts of the town where criminals were executed and buried. The ostler was left fully clothed, and a big crowd watched as a stake was driven through his body. They believed that the stake would prevent the person's spirit from rising up on Judgment Day. The body could then be laid to rest in the north or south side of a church graveyard. This brutal treatment of deeply troubled people was banned by an act of Parliament in 1832 following pressure from King George IV, but suicide or attempting it remained a criminal act until 1961.

By December 1760 the Inn was known as the Swan with Two Necks and Saracen's Head Inn. It had become the Higher Swan and Saracen's Head in 1767 when a disturbing advertisement appeared in the Manchester Mercury: 'Any gentleman or lady wanting to purchase a black boy, 12 years of age, with a good character, has had the small-pox and measles. Whoever this may suit may, by applying at the Higher Swan and Saracen's Head, in Market Street Lane, Manchester, meet with the proper person to deal with them on reasonable terms'.

People in Manchester began to protest against slavery and the slave trade in the late eighteenth century. Manchester Cathedral was packed to hear leading abolitionist, Thomas Clarkson, speak in 1787. The Act for the abolition of the slave trade was passed in 1807, followed by the 1833 Act for the abolition of slavery.

By 1767 a London carrier, Matthew Pickford, organised coaches from there on Wednesdays and Saturdays. Later in 1786, coaches set off daily, from Mr Pickford's warehouse opposite the Higher

Swan Court with Swan Lane to the left.

54

Keith Warrender

Edward Nobes was the licensee in 1969, with lunch-time and evening concerts

Swan and Saracen's Head, except Sundays, at 7am to Leeds and Liverpool. The last reference to the Higher Swan seems to have been in 1807 when the coach services to Liverpool and Leeds, then run by J Kawkwell & Co were transferred to the Palace Inn.

Swan Court

A watchman died in 1826 after a warehouse collapsed in Swan Court during improvement work. In 1829, three old houses adjoining the site of the former old Swan Inn were in a dangerous condition during work to extend the street.

Thomas Till opened premises in November 1848 on Market Street, with the entrance at 2 Swan Court, serving ales and stout, soups, chops and steaks. There were also two 'splendid' billiard tables.

Arcade Hotel

The hotel, on the corner of Swan Court and Market Street, was first owned by Miss Emily Nicholson. She and her sister Mary previously had refreshment rooms in the Exchange for many years. Miss Nicholson's Arcade Day Hotel and restaurant, 65A Market Street opened August 1867, with a luncheon bar. Miss Nicholson retired in 1874 and James Bebbington carried on the business which also contained smoke and billiard

rooms, and a ladies' room. Weddings and balls were held there, and they provided picnic food.

Liston's Bar

In November 1877 the Arcade Hotel was put up for sale, then following alterations and redecoration, it re-opened the following year as the Electric Hotel. By September 1879 the licence passed to John Greenhough, better known as Harry Liston, the entertainer (See chapter on Harry Liston). He renamed it Liston's Bar & Smoking Lounge but had moved on by 1881 and the bar was for sale in May 1882 .

DEATHS

In July 1900 two men were killed at Liston's Bar after the wooden balcony on which they were standing collapsed. They had been playing billiards and had gone to watch a parade going by on Market Street. They fell about 18ft amongst the crowds below and died later in hospital. At the inquest, it was reported the men had ignored the warning of a bar employee not to step onto the balcony as it was unsafe. A verdict of 'Accidental Death' was reached.

OLYMPIC SWIMMER

The bar was then owned by Richard Crawshaw and in 1903 he applied for a music licence. Alterations had to be carried out as part of the approval. The 1901 and 1911 censuses show that Crawshaw's son Robert was the manager. His widowed mother, Silence, was head of the household in 1911. The name had Puritan origins and came from a misinterpretation of the writings of St Paul.

Robert Crawshaw, born in Bury, was an Olympic swimmer and won a gold medal in the 1900 Paris Olympics with the British water polo team. He had been described by the New York Herald as the breast and backstroke champion of the world. Later he taught and gave swimming demonstrations around Manchester. In 1939 he was listed as a swimming teacher in Blackpool. Liston's Bar was granted a renewed music licence in 1914, despite police objections that within a radius of 300 yards of the bar there were already three houses with music licences, two cafés and a picture theatre. The room used for singing on the first floor was accessed by two narrow staircases. The tenant said the place was well patronised, with up to 1000 people present at various times on Saturday evenings. The lease had more years to run, and he had spent nearly £700 on structural improvements.

SUICIDE

The licensee, William Richardson, was fined £25 in 1919 after waiters were caught selling beer above the legal price limit. During the court proceedings it was stated that it cost £25 for hiring artistes on Saturdays. In the 1920s the cocktail bar and restaurant upstairs was regarded as a select venue. A barmaid died there in 1922 after drinking salts of lemon. The coroner gave a verdict of suicide after hearing of the troubled relationship with her husband. Harry Liston returned here in 1926 to take part in a concert. It is claimed that many soldiers were sent off in good heart from here to the wars in the Crimea, South Africa and France.

LESLIE STUART

Leslie Stuart, Manchester composer of 'Lily of Laguna', is said to have begun his singing career at Liston's. He was amongst the crowds at Central Station when Ferdinand de Lesseps, builder of the Suez Canal, visited Manchester in 1883. At the time Manchester was preparing a Parliamentary Bill for the construction of the Manchester Ship Canal. As the band played the 'Marseillaise' Stuart realised there was no

Liston's Bar in the 1940s, after repairs following war-time damage.

equivalent English marching song. Afterwards he went to Liston's bar, and sat at one of the tables to compose 'Soldiers of the Queen'. This later came to be regarded as the unofficial national anthem. Towards the end of his life, he returned after an absence of thirty years to perform at Liston's. A memorial plaque was presented to Manchester Libraries in 1939 which read: 'Leslie Stuart - 1866-1928 - a son of Lancashire who moved the nation to song... '

GEORGE FORMBY

In 1926, Liston's Bar came into the ownership of prominent Manchester Alderman, William Chapman JP, who planned to turn it into an 'inn de luxe'. Chapman was secretary of the Manchester Licensed Victuallers' Association and the proprietor of three licensed houses. He had been a member of the council for most of the years between 1907 and up to his death in 1944. Its nightly concerts drew big crowds with George Formby (snr) amongst the performers. Well-

The Snug Tavern

The beer and eating house was advertised to let in 1853 and located in a cellar in the buildings which later housed Liston's Bar. In 1884 the tavern was raided by the police, and Mary Pigott, the proprietor, and her two sons were amongst ten people arrested for illegal betting in a cellar. Mrs Pigott was fined £10, and her sons £25 each plus costs. In 1904

Robert Crawshaw's application to renew the licence was refused on the grounds of non-residence. His father, Richard, was the licensee of Liston's Bar above but was in poor health. Subsequently, Robert had been involved in its management, including supervising work on a new floor at Liston's.

Robert Crawshaw claimed the Snug was used as an eating house and that he slept there two or three times a week. This was not accepted by the Bench and it was commented that as a well-known swimmer (See 'Liston's Bar) he should not be sleeping in a damp cellar amongst the rats.

known stage people performed there under different names and it became an unofficial lunchtime club for visiting artists to the city. Young performers hoped they would be talent-spotted by theatre managers and agents.

WAR DAMAGE

Liston's Bar was badly damaged by incendiary bombs during the Blitz in December 1940, along with Ducie Chambers on Market Street. British Empire Chambers, opposite Liston's on the corner of Market Street and New Brown Street, was completely gutted. Further along Market Street the building on the corner of Corporation Street was also destroyed by enemy action. Harry Liston's music sheets and old visitors' books were amongst the items destroyed. It was one of 22 pubs seriously damaged, along with 23 public houses and breweries which were destroyed in the two days of bombing. A further 132 hostelries sustained lesser damage. 376 civilians and military personnel lost their lives and over 5000 people were made homeless.

The following Christmas Eve two bombers flew over Market Street. Horrified shoppers ran for cover as they saw the bomb doors open on the aircraft. In the panic one person was knocked down by a slow-moving car. However there were no further casualties or damage to buildings because the planes were British Whitley bombers dropping 10,000 leaflets from the police wishing everyone a merry Christmas and advising them on road safety. A prominent local politician said afterwards it had been unwise to make a drop at such a sensitive time without warning.

Liston's Bar was a popular place with visiting GIs. After the war its reputation went down and it became a haunt for criminals but the police intervened and it regained its earlier popularity. In 1958 music hall entertainment was restarted at Liston's with lunch-time and evening sessions introduced by a master of ceremonies in top hat and tails with the traditional gavel. The stage was open to all comers over the age of 18, and the early shows were packed to capacity. There used to be three bars, and a smartly-dressed commissionaire outside in Swan Court.

FINAL YEARS

The 'Pubs of Manchester' website had customers' memories of Liston's from the 1950s to the 70s. One remembered Eric the waiter with his blond streaks and quick service with drinks, and how the tables and chairs were bolted down to avoid being used during the many fights that broke out. Others recall the comedian Jackie Carlton performing there, and another went in as a 13 year old trying to sell newspapers to the drunk customers. Someone else related how he stood outside Liston's waiting for a friend to

exit the bar, and was told very forcibly by a lady to move on because he was ruining her business! The old bar closed on 21st March 1973 to make way for the new shopping centre and the farewell party was filmed by Granada TV. Stan Garside, a regular there, and a well-known pub pianist, played through the pub's final hours. Mrs Pamela Connor was the landlady at the time of its closure.

Top: Liston's Bar, Swan Court 1969. Below: Flower seller at the corner of Market Street and Swan Court.

©National Portrait Gallery, London

HARRY LISTON
The story of Manchester's greatest entertainer

Household name

Manchester-born Harry Liston was one of the greatest entertainers of his era and yet today he is little known. He was one of the longest-serving artists of music hall and variety, delighting audiences both in this country and abroad. His career from its beginnings in the 1860s spanned over sixty years. Although he has been rather overlooked and undervalued by later writers, it is clear from the reviews of his shows and the reminiscences of those who went to see him that he was held in great affection by the public.

He was a household name for many years and was always in demand. His supreme abilities with comic songs, acting and mimicry led to his being invited back to venues on numerous occasions and also requested to perform before royalty. At various times he was billed as 'The King of Entertainers' and 'The Nation's Premiere Entertainer'. He was a tall, striking figure and was said to be as cheery off-stage as he was on it. Minutes spent in his company were literally merry moments.

Early years

Harry Liston was born on the 3rd September 1843 at 10 Lime Street, Hulme, the eldest of seven children. Liston's real name was John Greenhough. It reads 'Greenhalgh' on one copy of his birth certificate, however, the family name had always been spelt 'Greenhough', and continued that way on registration certificates, listings, and the family grave stone.

Laban, John's father, was a baker and came from Sutton, Macclesfield. His wife, Elizabeth Derbyshire, was born in Worsley, and they were married in Manchester in 1842. They had originally lived in the High Town district but hit hard times and lived for a while in a cellar. It was assumed that John would follow his father into the bakery trade, but at the age of sixteen he probably realised the early starts and the heat of the ovens were not conducive to his singing career and he left the family business. From an early age he showed promise as a singer and reciter at school, and even rented an empty house with school friends to give shows for other youngsters in the district. The scenery was painted on newspapers and backlit to great effect with candles. They recited monologues such as 'Three-Fingered Jack' and 'The Miller's Tale'.

Greenhough's first appearance on stage was at the age of sixteen as a stooge for a stage hypnotist, possibly at Pendleton Town Hall. He gave such a convincing performance that even the hypnotist began to think he had genuinely put him into a trance. The following year, Greenhough got his big break when he was invited to sing one of his Irish songs at the concert of Will Townley, a popular Lancashire singer. This was at the Casino hall which later became the site of the Midland Hotel. The performance was warmly received until the audience realised he couldn't do an Irish jig and pelted him with apples and oranges. Afterwards, clog-dancer Tom Carroll taught him how to jig. At the time, Greenhough's day job was as a lithographic printer.

Greenhough married Elizabeth Proud on 21 December 1862 at Heaton

Liston's birthplace, Lime Street off Maple Street Hulme.

Harry Liston

where he performed at the Zoological Pleasure gardens' gala playing the comic character of Blue Beard. This was followed by a highly successful nineteen weeks of comedy at the Oxford Music Hall in Liverpool - his stage career was up and running.

Growing popularity

During 1864 he performed in Manchester, Leeds, Liverpool and Sunderland, then he made his London stage debut the following year. On 12th June 1865 he appeared at the Metropolitan Music Hall, Edgeware and then London's Royal Cambridge Music Hall. He was engaged by the Alhambra Palace where he stayed for two months. A review at the time read 'The great Harry Liston …has not been long in the Metropolis, but he has become exceedingly popular, as he deserves to be, if only on the score of his great originality'. He ended the year in pantomime at the Royal Colosseum, Liverpool.

Norris Parish Church. She was from Birmingham, and they were both living locally at the time. On the marriage certificate he was still listed as a printer. His brother-in-law George, also a printer, would later become part of his organisation. According to his daughter, Maude, Greenhough was a clerk at an iron works before he became a professional stage artist.

His stage name of 'Harry Liston' was given to him in July 1863 by the manager of the Scotia Music Hall in Glasgow. Greenhough turned up at the theatre and couldn't find his name on the poster and assumed he had gone to the wrong venue. However, further enquiries revealed that 'Harry Liston' at the top of the bill referred to him! The name had been selected because he reminded Mr Lofthouse, his mentor, of the great comic actor 'Liston'. From Glasgow, he went on to Liverpool

Harry Liston joined Arthur Lloyd's concert tour in 1866 where he was listed as a new comic vocalist. Later that year, he was billed as 'The Comique of Comiques' at Newcastle's Victoria Music Hall, where he performed his London Lion Comique act which was popular with audiences. This was the impersonation of an upper-class toff, which was also performed by other music hall artists including the notable Alfred Vance.

After his performance at the Cambridge Theatre in London in 1868, a reviewer wrote [Liston] is 'one of the youngest of the great comic favourites of his day, his popularity is very great.

The causes which contribute to his success are manifold. Mentioning only the most obvious of these, we observe that he sings and dances cleverly, talks amusingly, dresses suitably in character, and acts exceedingly well.' Another critic noted that Liston had a squint at his command that any comic singer would envy!

Whilst appearing in London, Liston was remembered for his lampooning of fellow comic George Leybourne, who used to go around London advertising his shows in a carriage drawn by four horses. Leybourne was famous for his rendition of 'Champagne Charlie,' and Liston attracted a lot of publicity by going around the streets in a humble cart pulled by four donkeys.

Around this period Liston was performing his memorable songs 'Dare Devil Dick', 'Nobody's Child' and possibly his greatest song at that point - 'Johnny I Hardly Knew Ye', receiving repeated calls for encores. It was sung to the the tune of 'When Johnny Comes Marching Home'. There has been much discussion about its origins. It was officially published in 1867 but Liston was singing it a year earlier. His version was probably a parody of a traditional song which dated back to the 18th century. By 1869, it was being used as a propaganda song by Irish Republicans.

'Merry Moments'

On 19th September 1868, Liston performed his first advertised show of 'Merry Moments' at Ashton Town Hall. He registered the title in 1868 and used it for the rest of his career. Others such as the McCarthy family had used the name but it became synonymous with his entertainments. He had discussed using the name with fellow performer Arthur Lloyd who had decided to use the tag-line 'Two hours of Fun' for his shows, so that the two entertainments wouldn't be confused. In the second 'Merry Moments' performance at Wigan Public Hall in December of that year, Liston introduced another significant line to his publicity. He stated that it would be 'Fun without vulgarity' - another feature which he retained to the end. He was not the only performer to make this claim but it was usually noted by the reviewers of his shows. Music hall could be quite bawdy so this ensured that his entertainment would appeal to all. Perhaps this also reflected his Sunday school upbringing, and he was later said to have been a church warden.

'Merry Moments' was essentially a theme in which to display his range of comic impersonations. He was one of the first 'one-man' shows with a pianist in support, although he sometimes had a company of singers in the programme. For example in a show at Cardiff in 1869, he sang eight songs in character, as well as doing impersonations of fellow artists Arthur Lloyd and George Leybourne. He was accompanied by three vocalists and a pianist. Books of his songs were on sale for sixpence at the venue which ensured many more would get

LISTON. — FREE-TRADE HALL.
THIS and EVERY EVENING, at Eight.
LISTON. The greatest success ever known in Manchester.
LISTON. The enormous concourse of visitors rightly proves
LISTON. the popularity of this versatile artiste.
LISTON. Vox populi and press proclaim Mr. Harry Liston the
LISTON. entertainer, par excellence, and award him the
LISTON. merit of being the best Mimic, Ventriloquist,
LISTON. Vocal Comedian, Instrumentalist, and Character
LISTON. Delineator extant.
LISTON. The Great Programme for this evening will include
LISTON. many New Impersonations, in addition to all
LISTON. the favourites, which have made his name a
LISTON. household word throughout the world.
LISTON. SPECIAL NOTICE. — The doors open at 7 30 this
LISTON. evening, and it is requested that all who are
LISTON. desirous of obtaining the best seats should avail
LISTON. themselves of the advantage of booking seats
LISTON. at the Box Office of the Hall, or of Forsyth
LISTON. Brothers.
LISTON. Overflow tickets issued on Saturday will be avail-
LISTON. able for this evening.
Performance commences at 8 and concludes at 10. Prices: 3s., 2s.,
1s., and 6d. RICHARD HOWARD. Manager.

1875 advertisement

to know of his work. The publicity added that the show would finish at a reasonable time for those who 'have a wholesome horror of late hours.'

On 8th March 1870 he performed 'Merry Moments' in Lincoln by Royal Command for the Prince of Wales, then the next month made his first appearance in Ireland at the Rotundo, Dublin. The local paper wrote 'As we anticipated, there was a crowded audience, who showed by their hearty laughter, still heartier applause, and almost too-frequent calls for encores, that their 'Merry Moments' with Harry Liston' were merry in the extreme. We have no hesitation in saying that this comic concert is the best of its kind that has been witnessed for many years in this city ...His accomplishments, too, are of a wider range than many, or indeed any in his line we have seen. He sings, dances and acts with remarkable ability, and possesses considerable talents as a ventriloquist and mimic.'

Liston's shows lasted two hours, although he sometimes performed a shorter version in two venues on the same evening. A Birmingham reviewer wrote that Liston kept the audience 'in a continual roar of laughter'. A man in the audience at a performance in Matlock laughed so much, he couldn't take any more and had to leave the theatre. There were so many things that attracted crowds back to his shows. He was a ventriloquist, and could also play unusual instruments such as the bellows, tin whistle and a wooden trumpet. Audiences marvelled at his quick changes of dress, facial transformations and his instant modifications in his voice from an adult to a child, or a humming insect to a singing bird. In addition to all of this, Liston composed many of the songs

Willow Publishing

'The Rustic Damsel' sung by Harry Liston in the character of Dismal Doleful from 1870, with slight variations on the words of T Dodsworth and J Holbrook.

in his act. He was also an outstanding impressionist, mimicking his fellow comedians.

He was acclaimed throughout Britain and received little criticism. However, one London correspondent thought his work was better suited to the provinces but Liston continued with great success on tours of the capital. The Manchester Guardian critic in 1872 said the impersonations were not original (although others commented on his originality), but with some reservations thought the entertainment 'clever and enjoyable'. Despite this critic's half-hearted review, Liston drew large crowds to the Free Trade Hall. The content of his shows was constantly changed and updated because he would be frequently asked back, although he would still repeat some of his most popular songs.

This review of his 1876 performance at the Surrey Street Music Hall, Sheffield is typical of the praise he received: '...even the most cynical must admit this gentleman's powers of amusing to be of the highest order. From the commencement of the performance to the conclusion, the spectator has presented to him a succession of scenes as varied as they are striking, as clever as they are original, and as well-executed as they are true to life. Vocal powers, musical ability, mimicry and ventriloquism are in turn exercised for the pleasure of the patrons...' Also in 1876 Liston and his family moved from 'Laurel Bank', Alexandra Road Manchester to the Recreation Hotel, Stalybridge - later renamed Liston's Hotel. Gustavus, their youngest son, was born there the same year.

MR. HARRY LISTON'S FAREWELL. M H. L. will fulfil only Three more Engagements before finally retiring from the Profession, viz., LLANDUDNO, 14th and 15th inst.; Manchester, August 25th, Six Nights; Winter Gardens, Southport, September 29th, Six Nights. Address, Bank-square, Southport.

Liston's first farewell in an 1879 advertisement, in the Era newspaper.

In January 1877 there came the surprising news that he was to retire from the stage and the announcement of 'farewell concerts'. He was still hugely popular and no reason for the decision was given at this time. It may have been to help look after his wife and children. Later that year he also introduced his new comedy drama 'Jack' in which, assisted by other actors, he played the roles of eight different characters. This was later adapted under the title of 'Slander' and was followed by a new two-act play 'Tricks' in 1878, again designed to be a showcase for his talents. Both 'Jack' and 'Tricks' were written by the notable comedy dramatist E Byam Wyke.

In August 1879 it was announced that Liston was to become the proprietor of the Electric Hotel in Manchester. As he prepared for retirement, he presented Mr J Justin, his secretary and musical director of six years, with a large gold signet ring for his services at his final concert in Manchester. He also dispensed with the services of his brother-in-law George. His plays including 'Slander' were made available for sale. In October, he went on his intended final tour of London, giving twice-daily performances of 'Merry Moments' at the Egyptian Hall in Piccadilly. London audiences had problems understanding his Lancashire dialect song 'Margery Daw' even though it had been popular around the country. After some thought, Liston re-presented it in a Somerset accent. From then onwards, he claimed, the song was sung and whistled throughout the capital.

Liston's Bar

The licence of the Electric Hotel at Swan Court and 65 Market Street had transferred from William Brigham to Harry Liston by September 1879. The business was re-named Liston's Bar and Smoking Lounge. Liston was a good host, and enjoyed sharing anecdotes from his stage career with the customers. He laid on a number of attractions including the provision, during winter lunch-time, of a tall brown jar of steaming hot-pot which was rapidly consumed. To encourage football supporters to come on Saturdays, he arranged for telegrams to be sent there with all the latest football results.

On one occasion, two men came into the bar behaving suspiciously and carrying a black bag. This was during the era of the Fenian bombings and Liston needlessly feared the worst. Then a customer thought that one of the men could be William Calcraft, the public executioner. This seems highly unlikely as Calcraft had retired some years earlier. However, Liston thought this was a good opportunity to attract customers and sent out runners to spread the news they had this

Allman Collection

Harry Liston and family 1876. Left to right: Frederick, Elizabeth with Gustavus, Albert, Harry with one of their twin daughters, and Harry Jnr.

controversial character on the premises and the bar quickly filled with drinkers. Despite his efforts the bar was not a financial success, and cost him his savings. He was listed as proprietor in July 1881 when the business was taken over by William Briggs, from the Regent Hotel in Salford. Liston was looking for new ventures, and it is thought he made an unsuccessful bid of £14,000 for Belle Vue Gardens - £1000 below the reserve price.

Family tragedy

During this period he continued with his 'farewell concerts'. But there was to be a great tragedy in his life. Liston had moved with his family to Brookside House, a large five-bedroomed detached house in Timperley, near Altrincham, and they had hired a domestic servant to assist with household duties. Their happiness was short-lived, with the death of his wife, Elizabeth, on 22nd August 1881. She was thirty eight and had been suffering from cirrhosis for some

time. Perhaps out of financial necessity, two days after her death he began accepting new bookings again for 'Merry Moments' and comedy dramas.

Re-marriage

1882 was to be another year of significant events. By the spring, Liston had moved out of Timperley and the house and contents were auctioned off. He also put on sale for £250, a glass bottle works he owned. Then on 1st June at St George's Church, Llandudno, he married actress Maude St Kilda, real name Eleanor White, from Bowdon. She appeared on stage with him for the first time in Derby. The previous year she had performed in an amateur drama in Harrogate. George, her father, had been a beer seller and provision dealer. He was from Lincolnshire, and his wife, Eliza, from Amsterdam. The next month, it was announced Liston was to become the proprietor of the Washington Hotel on the sea-front at Llandudno. On 4th August 1883 Eleanor gave birth to their daughter, Daisy. By then Liston's latest financial venture was in trouble. His business went into liquidation at the County Court of Carnarvonshire, and the hotel was auctioned. His stage work continued, and according to an advert for his show in Chesterfield in October, he had just returned from a 'foreign tour'. By this time he was being described in the Derby Daily Telegraph as a 'veteran', to which Liston objected. It was pointed out in a light-hearted reply to the newspaper that he was still under forty. The newspaper's editor explained the reference was in relation to his many years as an entertainer rather than his age!

His wife, a vocalist and pianist, re-joined him on stage and quickly gained positive notices. The following year she created the 'Animated Mummy' sketch for him which proved to be ever popular with audiences. In 1887 a reviewer described the routine as unlike anything done by other performers and 'a triumph of ingenuity

HARRY LISTON AT LONGRIDGE.—Harry Liston, the popular characteristic vocalistic, &c., gave his grand Jubilee entertainment in the Co-operative Hall, Berry-lane, on Monday evening, to a crowded audience. Though the price of admission was somewhat high, scores had to go away unable to find even standing room. For more than two hours the large concourse of people listened with evident delight, and, as the different characters were successfully imitated and pourtrayed in dress, voice, manners, &c., the people laughed and applauded again and again. Harry Liston is an orchestra, dramatist, vocalist, and elocutionist all rolled in one, and the rapidity with which he can change his dress is only equalled by his sparkling wit and humour. Whenever he cares to visit Longridge again we can promise him a hearty reception.

1887 review.

and whimsical invention'. That same year he was performing in an entertainment at the Crystal Palace watched by the Prince of Wales and members of royalty from around Europe. Liston announced in 1889, that he had received a lucrative offer to take his show to big cities in America but had to decline because of prior commitments. By 1889, Liston had taken over the former Theatre Royal Hotel on Talbot Road Blackpool and renamed it 'Harry Liston's Hotel'. He was listed there the following year

but again it was not a financial success. Liston later realized that its lavish furnishings put people off. In April 1890 he began his ninth annual successful engagement at the Opera Theatre, Crystal Palace. Later that summer he was out of action until October after breaking ribs whilst playing cricket.

During this period, tragedy struck again in his personal life, when his second wife Eleanor died in Ashton on Mersey, Sale on 17th September 1890. She was aged 34 and died from heart disease from which she had suffered during the previous year. Her final stage appearance had been in the preceding November.

New leading lady

Liston moved home again to Cottage Farm, Chinley, Derbyshire where he remained until about 1901. This address was used in his endorsement of Fletcher's indigestion mixture from 1896. He continued without a permanent leading lady until 1898 when he was joined by Louisa Lumley. He introduced her as his 'pupil' at Accrington Town Hall where they performed the comedy drama 'Married and Settled'. She was an instant success and remained with Liston for the next eighteen years.

In the same play later that year in Bradford, a reviewer said that Lumley 'showed herself possessed of distinct histrionic talent' and that 'the two artists kept the audience in a state of constant laughter.' She altered her stage name in 1899 to 'Miss Lord Lumley' and was described after their appearance at Leamington as a charming and graceful actress with a pleasing manner which quickly made her a favourite with the audience.

In September 1901 they gave an entertainment for Princess Leopold of Prussia and other members of royalty at the Victoria Hall Newquay.

Liston was off work for two months in 1908 with pneumonia. He had complained earlier in 1896 that sleeping in damp beds on tour made him ill. When he returned after his illness, he and Lumley gave the first performance of their new comedy duologue 'The First Baby' at Southport. Liston gave his address as Bland Street, Moss Side, Manchester in 1909; then in the April of that year, the Grey River Argus newspaper reported he was performing his 'Merry Moments' for a season in Christchurch New Zealand.

Liston's and Lumley's successful partnership continued and in 1913 they were presented with gold and silver gifts by the management of the Ripley Hippodrome after record-breaking attendances. By 1914 they were performing patriotic songs and sketches and in 1916 they entertained the wounded from the Great War at hospitals and Red Cross garden parties. They gave their final performance together with a selection from 'Merry Moments' in the August of that year.

'No time to grow old'

In 1917 Liston became the manager of the Rusholme Theatre on Wilmslow Road Manchester and was then only accepting occasional engagements. In 1920, aged seventy-seven, he joined the touring Edith Cavell concert party performing some of his 'Merry Moments'. The Stage newspaper reported that Liston at that age still had his audience in fits of laughter.

In May 1923 he appeared with the Veterans of Variety, then later that month a benefit matinee show at the Manchester Palace Theatre was given in his honour. This was supported by fellow performers and raised over £300 - the equivalent today of over £16,000. The theatre was packed as he stood on stage, still a slim upright figure looking considerably less than his eighty years, as he gave a short emotional speech. He and the other veterans were invited to a luncheon by

Liston and Sir Harry Lauder, in 1922.

the Lord Mayor the following day. In a 1922 newspaper interview, he said that even after entertaining for over sixty years, he still considered himself a young man with 'no time to grow old'. He always retained a positive attitude to life despite a number of personal setbacks.

During 1924 he toured the north of England and then announced he was planning a series of farewell shows. Harry Liston performed in

Allman Collection

Harry Liston in the dressing room at the Palace Theatre for the show given in his honour in 1923

Northampton and Tewkesbury in 1925, followed by two more shows at the Ardwick Picture Theatre and the Casino, Rusholme, after recovering from two unnamed accidents. He performed in the tea-time show on the BBC station 2ZY in June where he sang some of his most popular songs - 'Merry Moments', 'I'll Tell Your Wife', 'Smiling Tom', 'The Animated Mummy' and 'The Contented Irishman'. Probably his last public engagement was at a matinee in aid of the Artists' Benevolent Fund at Manchester in December 1926. He had been ill earlier in the year and had been hoping to resume his 'Merry Moments' engagements.

Someone who knew him saw him waiting in the street at All Saints, and reflected how alert and agile he seemed. Yet a few weeks later he passed away on the twenty-fifth of March 1929 aged eighty-six, at his home at 61 Ellesmere Street, Moss Side, with his daughter Maude present.

The funeral service at St James's Church Moss Side was conducted by his old friend Cannon Clark from Southport, whom he had known for fifty years after giving a performance for church funds. He was buried in the family grave at Weaste

Cemetery Salford. The Manchester Guardian wrote, 'He acted as boy, man and veteran. His death ends a career which was rich in good and mirthful things.'

An indication of how Liston, by then, was little known can be seen by the coverage in the local newspapers. The Evening Chronicle did not report his death but covered the interment, briefly describing him as 'the veteran Lancashire comedian'. The other Manchester evening paper made no mention of either his death or funeral, in spite of a family notice. The City News had an obituary, and several letters of appreciation of Liston in the following editions. His name lived on in the pub off Market Street, for many years known as 'Liston's Music Hall'.

Later writers on music hall either give few details or completely ignore Liston's career. Yet he was clearly regarded by those who used to go to shows of the period as being one of the music hall 'greats' alongside fellow comedians Arthur Lloyd, George Leybourne, Fred Macabe and Alfred Vance. Surely it is time for the achievements of this talented Manchester entertainer to be recognised with a plaque somewhere in the city.

Merry Moments

Sung by Harry Liston

A hearty good laugh is food for the mind,
Proclaim it at once to the world and mankind,
And in my humble efforts I hope you will find
    That laugh in my 'Merry Moments'.
I'll try to make fun without a rude jest,
My honour's at stake, I am put to the test,
And your kind attention at once I request,
  Just for my 'Merry Moments'.

  CHORUS - My maxim through life
  Is to keep clear of strife;
Help my friend, no ill will bear opponents.
  Be jolly all day
  In a moderate way;
Make each hour of life 'Merry Moments'.

Now whilst on a visit to this very town,
To an old friend of mine, whose name it is Brown,
Whose daughters are charming, I really must own,
    For with them I've spent 'Merry Moments'.
At noon in the garden, I'd oft go to sleep,
Those mischievous girls in my presence would creep,
Black my face, and my coat tails pin fast to a seat,
But yet they were all 'Merry Moments'.

  CHORUS

Doing good actions each day of my life,
Hearing sweet music, 'Piano or Fife,'
Or snugly at home with a dear little wife,
    All these are 'Merry Moments'.
Merry examples I'll give you a bunch,
Either eating your dinner, your supper, or lunch,
Reading your 'Fun,' or drinking your 'Punch'
    All of them are 'Merry Moments'.

  CHORUS

I hope on my travels to call here next year,
And see once again all my patrons now here,
And hear you all say without any fear,
    That you've enjoyed my 'Merry Moments'.
A few types of character at once I'll portray,
The rich and the poor, the grave and the gay,
And if you are pleased why then I must say
That they are mutual 'Merry Moments'.

  CHORUS

Harry Liston 1899.

The Liston connection

As already mentioned, Harry Liston was named after John Liston (1776-1846) the most celebrated comedian of his generation. Throughout Harry Liston's career on stage, there were other Listons around. First and foremost was fellow performer Victor Liston, also a comedian and mimic. He was popular though not regarded by some as being as good as Harry. He began on stage before Harry and was irritated that people thought they were related or that he was copying him. His most famous song was 'Encore! Encore! Encore!' He died in 1913.

There was also William Henry Liston, lessee and manager of the Olympic and other theatres who died in 1876. Some newspapers wrongly printed his name as 'Harry' prompting Harry Liston to put out a newspaper notice stating he was not dead yet and was appearing that evening in Preston.

Another artist, a Mr Beaumont, performed under the name of Harry Liston about 1890 until he was threatened with legal proceedings.

Harry Liston on tour - rats, fires and explosions

Liston paid for a town crier to announce one of his shows, and overheard what he said while out walking down the high street. '... He is a gread man, and was never be in Barmouth before. He is there tonight at half-past seven. If you leave it till tomorrow, it will be too late. If you go late, you have only to look ad them outside'.

During the performance of 'Parted' in West Bromwich, Maude St Kilda, at the end of one of the acts, had to throw a novel at the villain of the play. The actor was standing too close to the naked flames of the footlights and the book landed on one of the footlights and caught fire. Miss St Kilda, seeing the danger of the theatre going up in flames, rushed forward and grabbed the burning book, narrowly avoiding the descending act-drop, and stamped out the flames.

An incident in Altrincham in 1891 illustrates how convincing were the many characters which Liston rapidly transformed into during his performances. He gave his Altrincham landlady a complimentary ticket for his show but afterwards she complained she had not seen much of him on stage except as compere. She questioned why the other fourteen members of the company were not lodging with her, not realising they were all Harry Liston characters.

Liston and company found themselves with no accommodation while in Newquay during a bank holiday week. Everywhere was fully booked and they had to sleep in the dressing rooms of the Victoria Hall where they were performing.

He was booked to give a show in Flint, and during the day, a lady's eccentric antics in the street caused a crowd to gather. People thought she needed medical attention until someone shouted wrongly, 'Let her go! It's Harry Liston in disguise advertising tonight's programme'.

Willow Publishing

HARRY LISTON,
The Royal Humorist,
HOPES YOU WILL . . .
HAVE "MERRY MOMENTS"
IN 1905. . *March* 4

On a trip to Paris, he asked the hotel concierge for a room in his best French. To his amazement they replied 'Why, blime, if it aint 'Arry Liston all the w'y from London!'

He and Miss Lumley stayed overnight in an old farmhouse just outside Manchester while on tour. In the morning, Lumley came out of her room with horrifying accounts of a rat. The landlady confirmed the presence of rats and turned to her daughter and asked how long ago was it since it had bitten someone's ear off.

At the time of performing 'Dare Devil Dick' in Liverpool, Liston kept a box which contained wigs and magnesium paper, presumably for theatrical effects, in the dressing room. The magnesium somehow accidentally caught fire and exploded. These were the times of Fenian riots and Liston found himself nearly arrested for trying to blow up the hall.

Just before going on stage in Nottingham, Liston received a telegram 'Come at once - father dying'. A big audience had assembled to see him and so he went on with the performance with some difficulty before returning to his father.

While coming to the end of singing 'Nobody's Child' at a hall in Galway the temporary floor boards collapsed and he disappeared along with the pianist under the stage. The audience let out a delighted shout of 'Haroo that's grand'. Liston and his accompanist managed to free themselves from under the collapsed piano. Liston got back on stage to a chorus of cheers and announced 'Ladies and gentlemen, this will be repeated tomorrow night!' The following evening in front of a crowded hall he did repeat the song but managed to exit in conventional fashion - much to the disappointment of the audience.

Liston in Court

Liston sued Philip Brame at Manchester County Court in a dispute over tickets for two concerts he gave in aid of the Little Sisters of the Poor. The entertainment took place at the Free Trade Hall Manchester in March 1876 with Liston agreeing to split the ticket proceeds with the organiser. However, Mr Brame, representing the charity, refused to hand over a percentage of money taken from tickets issued by Liston's manager Mr Howard. The court found in favour of Liston and he was awarded £35.

In 1879 there was a similar case involving Liston and the management of the Southport Winter Gardens. Liston had been entitled to half the ticket receipts but the Southport management had made deduction from half of the proceeds of complimentary tickets provided by Liston. Again it was ruled that the management had no right to make the deduction and he was awarded costs. Perhaps more interesting are the details revealed in court of the amount Liston earned from the week of concerts. His share of the takings was £61.07 - which today would be worth about £8,800.

In 1881 Liston gave evidence at Lancaster during the trial of a fifteen-year old who had stolen various items belonging to him.

His belongings had been stored in a dressing room at the music hall where he had performed. The youth, who worked at the hall, had removed from Liston's trunk a manuscript music book, his famous bellows, a large quantity of his sixpenny music books, three song books and other items of property. Liston had moved to the next venue before he realised that some of his stage props and other possessions were missing.

The police in Lancaster searched the youth's lodgings where they found most of Liston's property half-hidden behind a chest of drawers. The lad, George Sloper, claimed he had taken the things for safe-keeping and was intending to send them on to Liston. His story was not accepted by the Bench and he was sentenced to a month's hard labour at Lancaster prison.

Liston was summoned to the Rotherham West Riding Court in March 1903. He had given a show at a local school at Rawmarsh under the auspices of the local cricket club. Police sergeant Hustler, who came to the performance, deemed that they were 'stage plays' for which the cricket club was not licensed. The charge against Liston was of performing on an unlicensed stage. Liston argued he had performed these sketches at hundreds of places around the country without hindrance. The Bench ruled a stage licence was required and he was ordered to pay costs.

The Wilton Club

The social club at 9/11 New Cannon Street was established in 1878 for card playing and billiards. It was originally based in Cromford Court before moving to New Cannon Street 1882. Many expected it to be part of the 1885 police raid on many betting clubs in Manchester (See Hodson's Square) but it continued as normal on the day of the raid without any interference. The building was designed by William Gunson, whose other work included Lytham Pier and Pavilion, Buxton Gas Works, and Hyde Reform Club. The club became a cabaret venue in the 1960s.

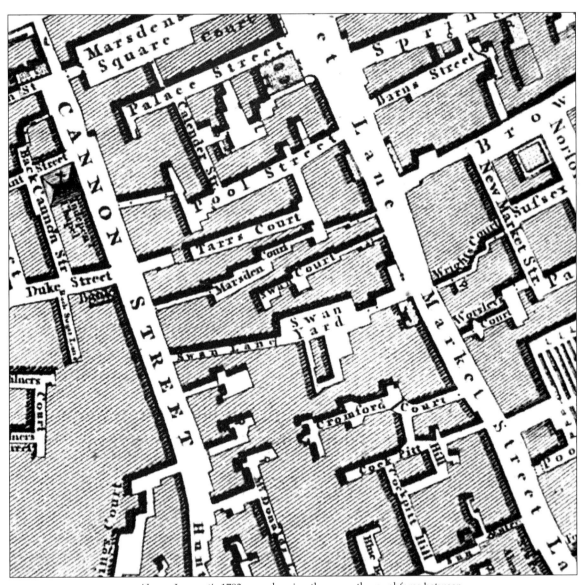

Above: Laurent's 1793 map showing the many thoroughfares between Market Street and Cannon Street. There were a number of street changes later, including Tarr's Court being extended to become New Brown Street, and Swan Yard and Swan Lane into New Cannon Street. Opposite page: New Cannon Street off Market Street in 1969.

Market Street c1900

Note the two KINO signs on the building just above the first horse-drawn tram. This is Wilton Chambers which was replaced by the Ceylon Café (See page 76).

The Kino brothers, James Edward, Alfred and Isador, at 35-37 Market Street began trading as merchant-tailors in Manchester in 1878. They were of Polish origin when the country had been annexed by Russia. In 1881, they advertised themselves as 'the celebrated London tailors offering the latest fashions in ladies' and gentlemen's garments.' They were also naval and military outfitters.

The brothers opened further businesses in Glasgow, London, Leeds and Bradford with varying degrees of success. Isador later withdrew from the partnership, then in 1893, as a result of the twenty-week long Lancashire cotton strike, they got into financial difficulty. Their weekly sales went down from £300 to £160 which was not sufficient to cover their costs and they were declared bankrupt. The Kinos emigrated to Australia where they continued to have business problems.

The premises on Market Street were later occupied by the Grand Clothing Company.

Keith Warrender

THE CEYLON CAFÉ

The Ceylon Café at 35 Market Street opened in October 1904. It advertised the new café as providing 'high-class refreshments at popular prices' serving French pastries and Vienna bread. The café had ladies' rooms, smoking rooms, and a string orchestra. In its heyday, the café had four floors which could accommodate 1000 people. The waitresses were known as 'nippies', and an eight-piece orchestra entertained the customers. During WWII the café was self-service.

The new building replaced Wilton Chambers and was designed by Manchester architects Charles Heathcote and Sons and WA Thomas of Liverpool. The café company was in existence by 1900 in Sheffield and also had cafés in Liverpool, and Leeds. Charles Heathcote designed a number of Manchester's finest commercial premises,

while Walter Thomas, one of the great Liverpool architects, designed the iconic Royal Liver Building. This was one of the first multi-storied buildings of reinforced concrete. Thomas was offered a knighthood for his work but declined because of his dislike of publicity.

The design of the Ceylon Café was different from the surrounding buildings and not to the liking of some architectural experts. Nikolaus Pevsner described it as a 'Saracen joke' in 1967. Professor Charles Reilly, in a series of articles on Manchester architecture for the Guardian, wrote in 1924: 'Architectural decency and western civilisation are thrown to the dogs ... number 35-37 is a modern terra-cotta glazed structure in an Earl's Court brand of Turkish architecture. Five glazed minarets rise from the second floor with cement towers behind them. Beware the balconies and horseshoe windows of pantomime. Unless Market Street is definitely on an amusement park, such a building is not a little unfair to the neighbourhood. Messrs Lyons however, who occupy it, seem not too displeased for they have put their name around it in gilt letters.'

Whilst it is true the new building didn't blend in with the surrounding property, the architects had been briefed to design it in eastern style. The Ceylon Café Company had branded their establishments as 'luxury with economy'. They were designed with lavish interiors of Persian marble, Serpentine dados, deep carpets and many large mirrors.

Following the success of the café in Market Street, the company, which reputedly began in London, engaged the two original architects to work on a similar design for the State Restaurant at Piccadilly which opened in 1906. The Ceylon Café Company later that year opened a café at 1 Princess Street, Albert Square and moved from 35 to 74 Market Street in 1907. A further branch on Deansgate was also opened. After making a profit of over £25,000 in 1909 they were taken over by J Lyons and Co who were expanding into the provinces. The two companies had earlier links, with the Ceylon Café Company, agreeing to restrict their business to the provinces in exchange for investment from Lyons in 1902. Joe Lyons' tea shop on Market Street closed in 1964.

Above: Lyon's café, Piccadilly designed in a similar Moorish theme to the Ceylon Café.
Left: Lyon's Café in the premises of the former Ceylon Café, Market Street.

Above: Congested Market Street at the junction with Corporation Street and Cross Street.

Left: Market Street c1923, with Dunn & Co on the corner of Cromford Court.

Opposite page, top: Market Street c1925

Opposite page, below: Walmsley Brothers' outfitters shop had cellars from which there was said to be a vaulted brick passageway which once led up Market Street, and towards the Cathedral in the other direction. No official inspection was made but it may have been the remains of an old sewer which ran into the River Irwell.

GREENWOOD'S BUS OFFICE

Greenwood's bus office waiting room and parcel room was at 31 Market Street. John Greenwood has been called the 'Father of Road Transport' after starting Britain's first horse-drawn omnibus service in Manchester in 1824. A similar service began in London five years later. Greenwood had expected to become a miller but an accident with a gun damaged his hand and he became a toll-collector. He was the joint toll-keeper at the fork of the road between Eccles Old Road and Bolton Road, Pendleton, and realised the potential of public transport to and from Manchester.

Greenwood opened his pioneering business between the old maypole on the village green at Pendleton and Market Street, Manchester. It was the first to pick up and set down passengers on request with no prior booking needed. The first bus was a type of hackney carriage pulled by a horse but this was soon replaced by coaches described as square boxes on wheels, with about nine seats inside and four outside next to the driver, and known as 'The Bees'. Greenwood often boasted he had taught Manchester people to ride and to lose the use of their legs.

The driver not only had to hold a whip to control the horse but also a horn to announce the presence of the bus. When a stop was requested, he opened the door to let passengers off and collect the fare, which was 6d inside and 4d outside. Greenwood had problems with drivers who did not declare their true takings when they got back to the office at Pendleton. However he seemed to get what he was rightfully owed when he raised his loud voice and used a few expletives. Greenwood wore yellow corduroy knee breeches and a white shirt and was often seen outside the office smoking a long clay pipe.

Later he added services to Buxton, Chester and Sheffield as well as to other parts of Manchester as the city expanded. In the early days of the omnibuses, there was something of a free-for-all between the various companies and Greenwood was fined several times for running services on routes for which he didn't hold a licence. At his death in 1851 his son of the same name took over the company, including the toll contract which brought in £200,000 a year before turnpikes were abolished. The local MP, Joseph Brotherton of Pendleton, died on one of the Greenwood buses in 1857 while travelling into Manchester with friends.

John Greenwood jnr. became manager of the Manchester General Conveyance Company, which was formed in 1858 to co-ordinate the services of all the omnibus companies. By then 1200 horses were being used. In 1862 he took the new longer three-horse buses to London, at the time of the Great Exposition, to rival the smaller local buses. The company continued in operation until 1903 after going through several mergers and the setting up of a municipal organisation in 1901.

Horse-drawn bus at the Greater Manchester Museum of Transport

'Barbarian' on the omnibus

An indignant letter to the Manchester Guardian in 1853 highlighted the sometimes unpleasant experience of travelling on Greenwood's omnibuses. The correspondent had been journeying into Manchester one evening when a man smoking a cigar got on. The smoke and the fumes in the confined space soon became unpleasant and the gentleman sitting next to him asked him to put out the cigar. The man refused, saying he had permission from the conductor, so the passengers, including seven ladies on their way to a concert, had to endure the 'effluvia arising from the imperfect combustion of cabbage and tobacco leaves'. The writer added 'There can be no objection to any person enjoying a cigar, or a beef-steak, or a game of leap-frog, if so disposed; but I don't think an omnibus a very suitable locality for such amusements... The new omnibuses are a great convenience; let us keep them so, despite the inroads of barbarians.'

LOWER SWAN INN

In one of the earliest references to the inn, Deville Desaubrys was publicising his dancing school for ladies, gentlemen and children at the Swan with Two Necks, Market Street Lane. The advertisement in November 1760 indicated he had taught there before. He lived in Liverpool but gave lessons in Manchester up to 1767.

Richard Turnock announced various services of carrier wagons or carriages starting from the Lower Swan With Two Necks in March 1762. The following year, John and Martha Upton, late of the Old Boar's Head, Hyde's Cross, took over the Lower Swan With Two Necks from Christopher Nixon. It had been 'very genteelly fitted' for gentlemen, tradesmen etc. There were good lodging-rooms with good beds, a good stock of wines and liquors and stabling for large numbers of horses. They also had a large yard and warehouse for tradesmen.

HEAD OF ENTERTAINMENT

George Alexander Stevens stayed at the Swan Inn in 1764 to give his new amusing and entertaining lecture on heads and head-dresses, promising to give 'a belly-full of laughs'. Tickets for the two-hour monologue cost two shillings. He had first performed it earlier in the year at the Little Haymarket Theatre in London with great success.

He stood behind a long table covered in green cloth on which were many papier mâché busts and wig blocks. The characters were a cross-section of society from a Billingsgate fishwife to a Methodist minister. Stevens selected each one to make satirical comments about them. This was the era of the growing popularity of satire with the emergence of artists such as Cruikshank, Hogarth, Gillray and Rowlandson. He is thought to have been inspired by a man's description of local worthies, and he also worked with a puppet-maker who presented a one-act satirical puppet show.

Stevens, born in London 1710, became an actor and toured this country and North America with his presentation. He gave further lectures in Manchester between 1765 and 1779, and nationally delivered an estimated thousand lectures which were said to have earned him £10,000. He later devised other versions of the presentation but none was as popular as the original. Many others imitated his lecture but as there were no copyright laws at that time he was unable to prevent them.

He was also a novelist, playwright, poet and writer of hundreds of drinking songs. He later lost his considerable fortune through poor business decisions and was put in the debtors' prison at Yarmouth. Despite his difficult circumstances, he was able to write a witty letter from his cell explaining how various items of clothing, wig and footwear paid for his meals and well-being while incarcerated. He died in Biggleswade, Bedfordshire in 1784 predicting, two weeks before, the precise day of his death. A book of his works was later published, including his celebrated lecture on heads.

CURING DISTEMPERS

Bardwell Shappee was also at the Lower Swan in 1764 treating patients. He was an unqualified doctor who had been a pupil of his uncle, Dr Shappee, for 14 years. He said that he was allowed to practise under an act of parliament. After thirty years of attending to people he claimed he could cure most 'distempers' of the body. He asserted surgeons considered him to be 'the wonder of the age', curing thousands of ruptures, 'broken bellies' and 'falling wombs'. His treatments had been reported in London and provincial newspapers. Shappee was also a 'man-midwife' as a growing number of male doctors, rather than female mid-wives, began attending births in the early 1700s. Unfortunately he couldn't cure his own gout and travelled around the country because the exercise helped to ease his condition. He first came to Manchester in 1758 when he stayed at the Old Boar's Head, Hyde's Cross. He promised complete confidentiality stating: 'All secrets of both sexes are kept by the doctor. He does not so much ask from whence they come, or where they go.' The gentry could be visited at home. His last reported visit to Manchester was in 1766.

The Irish Giant

Patrick Cotter O'Brien (1760-1806) could be seen at the Lower Swan in November 1784 for the price of a shilling. At eight feet and one inch tall, he was known as the 'Irish Giant'. The former bricklayer came to Bristol in 1779 and made his living as a fairground attraction and at other venues.

He came to Manchester on four occasions, and on his last visit in 1802, he reassured everyone that they were not seeing his ghost, as newspapers had been regularly reporting his death. He enjoyed walking around the town at midnight when the streets were deserted and lighting his pipe from the street oil lamps.

Before he died in Bristol he requested in his will that his body should be left untouched, however it was exhumed three times. During the 1972 exhumation a detailed examination of his skeleton was carried out. Finally in 1986 his remains were cremated after being moved for building redevelopment.

SCHOOL OPENED

In 1768 Alexander Dassti opened his school at the Lower Swan teaching French and German, fencing and the violin. He also offered a translation service. He had begun the school in 1766 at a house on Deansgate and at that time he was living in Liverpool. By 1772 he was listed as a merchant, dealer and pedlar but had been declared bankrupt. Coaches started off from Richard Dixon's Lower Swan in 1781 at 2pm for Blackpool on Mondays, Wednesdays and Fridays, for 13s 6d inside and 8s 6d outside. A coach left for London at 3.30pm on the same three days. Coaches also set off from here to Birmingham, Hull, Lancaster and Carlisle.

THE ACTOR'S SKULL

In December 1783, George Frederick Cooke, a notable actor of his time, stayed at the Lower Swan and made the first of many appearances in Manchester until he left for New York in 1810. He died there in 1812, and eight years later his body was removed to another part of the grave-yard while a memorial stone was being added to his grave. During this process, the skull of the dead actor was stolen. It came into the possession of a New York doctor who loaned it out to a theatre company who were performing Hamlet.

CLOSURE

Following the death of Richard Dixon (Snr), the Lower Swan Inn was advertised to let by his widow, Sarah, in 1796. From the advertisement we get an idea of the impressiveness of the inn. It was described as an elegant mansion with fifty bedrooms, with stabling for a hundred horses and 'equalling any inn in the north of England'. Nathaniel James became the next landlord until his retirement in 1799 and then it was announced that the premises of the Lower Swan were to be demolished to make way for warehouses. Richard Dixon and Thomas Bowman thanked their customers for their patronage over twenty years, and stated they would continue the business from the coach office of the Upper Swan Inn, with coaches leaving daily at 8am for Liverpool

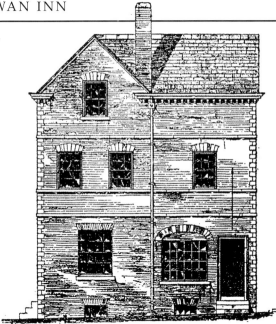

Reconstruction of the Swan coach office for the 1887 Manchester Jubilee Exhibition.

Scatchard & Hardy, tea merchants, opened a shop in front of the Old Lower Swan, Market Street Lane in 1800. Twelve years later the shop and other buildings, including the Lower Swan Inn and premises formerly used as the coach office, were auctioned. Up to twenty mail and other coaches continued daily from the Swan Inn coach office operated by J Weatherall and R Cookson, which they rented from Edward Baines at the Swan Inn.

In October 1828 an inquiry was held at the Blackfriars Inn to compensate Edward Baines, occupier of the Swan Inn on Market Street for 25 years. The premises were about to be partly demolished in preparation for the Market Street Improvements following an Act of 1821 which empowered the Commissioners to enlarge and widen Market Street. Work had begun two years previously and the street had been excavated by the highway surveyors to about six feet below the level of the Inn, which resulted in difficult access and loss of business. Baines was awarded £900 compensation for loss of earnings. The following May workmen began pulling down the buildings. The coach offices remained until about 1838.

MANCHESTER, February

This present FRIDAY Evening,
And to-morrow Evening SATURDAY,
And positively no longer.

1767

At Mr. DIXON's, the Swan Inn, Market-street-lane,

Mr. SAUNDERS,

The celebrated EQUILIBRIST, from the Theatres Royal, in London, Dublin, and Sadler's-Wells, Will Entertain the Ladies and Gentlemen, with a variety of New and Astonishing Equilibriums on The

SLACK WIRE,

Without a Pole, never attempted by the *Turk*, Mr. *Maddox*, Mr. *Matthews*, Miss *Wilkinson*, or any other Person but by
Mr. S A U N D E R S.

Among a Variety of new and astonishing Equilibriums, Particularly he will Balance TWO CHILDREN at once on the Wire in full Swing. He will imitate the Macaroni Tails, with a Stick and Hat. He will Balance a Pyramid of GLASSES, illuminated with Lights, in a Brilliant Manner.
Particularly he will stand on his HEAD upon the Foot of a

DRINKING GLASS,

Without holding with his Hands, and at the same time will discharge a Brace of PISTOLS, the Wire being in full Swing, to the Surprize of every Beholder. On Account of the great number of new Performances Mr. SAUNDERS will divide this Exhibition on the Wire into Two Acts, between which he will Balance

A Mighty Giant standing upon the Top of
a L A D D E R,

Mr. SAUNDERS will Entertain the Ladies and Gentlemen, with several select AIRS and favourite TUNES on a NEW COMPLETE SET of the so much admired

MUSICAL GLASSES.

Miss MARIANNA from ITALY;
Who will Perform LOFTY and GROUND TUMBLING.
SIEUR REA, Junior,

Will Exhibit several new PHISOLOPHICAL EXPERIMENTS, MATHEMATICAL OPERATIONS, and MAGICAL DECEPTIONS.

The Original DANCING DOG,

Whose FEATS, cannot be equalled by any other DOG in the WORLD.
TO CONCLUDE, WITH A CURIOUS PIECE OF

M A C H I N E R Y,

From the City of ROME.
FRONT SEATS ONE SHILLING.——BACK SEATS SIX-PENCE.
The DOORS to be opened at SIX, and the Performance to begin at SEVEN each EVENING.

Samuel Saunders came to the Lower Swan Manchester in 1767 on a tour of Britain.
He was from a travelling fairground troupe family and performed for the Royal family
in 1760 and for King Louis XVI in 1786. 'Miss Marianna from Italy', a five-ft tall
automated figure, made two later appearances at the Swan.

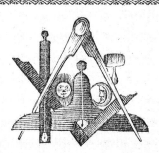

THE UNPARALLELED
IRISH GIANTS.
THE MOST SURPRISING GIGANTIC
TWIN BROTHERS,

Who had the Honour to be seen by their Majesties, and the Royal Family, at Windsor in the Year 1784, with great Applause; being the only Tall Men that his Majesty ever honoured with that Compliment.

ARE JUST ARRIVED

And to be Seen at Mr. DIXON's, the LOWER-SWAN INN,
MARKET-STREET-LANE, MANCHESTER,

These truly amazing Phænomena are indisputably the most astonishing Production of the human Species ever beheld since the Days of

GOLIAH;

As has been sufficiently demonstrated from the repeated Approbation of the first Personages in this Kingdom, as well as Foreigners of Distinction; from several of whom they have had the most pressing Invitations to visit their respective Courts.

THESE AMAZING
COLOSSUSES
Are but TWENTY-FOUR YEARS OF AGE,
AND VERY NEAR
EIGHT FEET HIGH.

Nor does that amazing Size more agreeably surprize the curious Spectator, than their Proportion in every Respect to their stupendious Height; a Circumstance so seldom to be found in any extraordinary Production of Nature.

Ladies and Gentlemen are respectfully informed, that the Hours of Admittance are from Ten in the Morning till Two in the Afternoon, and from Three till Nine at Night.——Their Stay will be but Short.

ADMITTANCE, Ladies and Gentlemen 1s.——Servants, &c. 6d.

Broadsheet advertising the arrival in 1787 of the Knipe brothers, known as the Irish Giants, at the Lower Swan Inn. They were said to be the tallest-ever identical twins at 7ft 2ins tall. They were from County Derry; their cousin Charles Byrne's height was 7ft 7ins.

The Cockpit tower is in the centre, whilst the tower on the right is St Ann's Church in this 1728 print.

COCKPIT HILL

The earliest reference to cock fighting in Manchester was on a strip of land between Hunt's Bank and the Irwell, in 1475. There was a further indication of cockfighting in 1623 when a parcel of land called 'Cocker Field' Manchester was purchased by John Moxon, a hosier. It would have been the location of this activity before a cockpit was built. Cockfighting was the gruesome spectacle of two roosters fighting to the death, with bets being taken.

The 1650 map of Manchester shows the domed cockpit building at Cockpit Hill with a narrow lane leading up to it from Market Place. The dome of the cockpit is also to be seen in a 1728 panorama of Manchester. The barbarous practice of cockfighting was once a popular sport, with the Earl of Derby a frequent participant in the betting here. Even boys from the nearby Grammar School went along. Later, cockfighting began at Broughton Road, Salford, about 1812. Cockfighting was officially banned in 1835 but it still went on at Newton in 1840 and Bolton in 1846.

Henry Dickanson of Salford owned lands around Cockpit Hill in 1739. An old detailed plan showing his properties of that era was seen by the Guardian newspaper in 1854. Sadly, the plan drawn by Joseph Hill is not listed in any public archive collections today. Do any readers know of its whereabouts? The Guardian gave a precise description of the plan which also included details of underground tunnels and drains, as well as indicating a now long-forgotten water source which ran through the district. There was a three-ft wide drainage tunnel along part of the south side of Market Stead Lane, and various drains leading into it from nearby properties.

The newspaper writer described a cartway leading up to Cockpit Hill where the square Cockpit House was situated. To the south and west were houses with kitchens, and to the north several courts and houses including an inn. Beyond lay a large garden with a 'summer bower'. Fifty years after the map was made, Cockpit Hill led into Cromford Court.

Cockpit Hill from Sun Entry.

Grimshaw's Pie House

Grimshaw's pie house at 14 Cockpit Hill was fondly remembered by many locals. It had been run by the family since 1766 and was situated in one of two cottages where they lived. George Grimshaw married Susanna Wignall in 1784 and she continued the business after her husband's death.

The oval veal pies were a favourite of employees in the surrounding warehouses and cost four pence. Sam Bamford, the writer and reformer, recalled receiving a free meal, including the use of a knife and fork, by making complimentary remarks about Susanna's daughter - a concession not offered to many others.

Another customer recalled going to the pie house on a dark evening. In the glimmer of the street lamps it was easy to believe that kidnappers and other criminals could be lurking in these dark alleys and narrow streets.

By 1828 ownership of the shop had passed to the Wignall family. From 1842 it was also licensed to sell alcohol. The passageway to it from Market Street was known as Pie Entry until its closure in 1962. In 1854 the pie house business moved to Smithy Door. It was managed by Mrs Ellen Blackley, formerly Wignall, who was the niece of the late Mrs Grimshaw. The business closed about 1864.

THE FATTED CALF

The beerhouse was built about 1855 on or close to the site of Grimshaw's pie house and in 1859 named appropriately the Fatted Calf after previously selling veal pies. It was owned by William Wignall who was born in Moston in 1811. He moved to Hulme where he acquired other properties, and came to Cockpit Hill about 1858. In 1860 the beerhouse was still being advertised as 'Grimshaw's original pie house, selling superior wines, cordials, ales, porter, cider and perry'. By the following year it was 'The Fatted Calf, at 14 Cockpit Hill'.

After Wignall's death in 1864 his son, also called William, took over. In 1866 he applied for a spirit licence for his dining and refreshment rooms. He claimed 80 people dined there daily, and that they could accommodate up to 200. By 1868 it was advertised as 'Wignall's Chop and Sandwich Rooms'. The inn became popular with workers from the Guardian and Examiner newspapers who came for supper between 11pm and 1am, but Wignall was refused an extended licence. Wignall also owned the Grotto beerhouse at Cockpit Hill, the Nelson Vaults on Oldham Road and the

Talbot Hotel in Moss Side. But in 1882 he was in financial trouble with debts of £25,000 and declared bankrupt. He died suddenly at the Fatted Calf in 1889. By 1891 his daughter Ellen held the licence in partnership with Mary Leak until 1892 when Miss Leak took over the licence and ownership. She married chemical manufacturer Samuel Anderson and the pub remained in family ownership until it was auctioned in 1917.

In 1929 nine people were affected by a gas leak at the hotel, including the licensee Frank Worthington and his wife. Employee Madge Fitton had been woken up by her alarm at 7.30am to find her room filled with gas. She raised the alarm and found a colleague unconscious in the next room. Madge managed to drag her to a window. Another member of staff had to make her way down five flights of stairs before collapsing in Pie Entry. A cleaner at neighbouring Cromford House and a waitress at a cafe in Corporation Street were also found unconscious. Five people were taken to the Manchester Royal Infirmary, including a police officer and a gas department employee. A cordon was put round the affected buildings, and smokers in the vicinity were ordered to put out pipes and cigarettes. The leak was thought to have been caused by sagging gas pipes. But for the prompt action of Madge Fitton, aged 23, there would have been fatalities.

Although just a few yards off Market Street, the pub could only be accessed by the narrow Pie Entry or back streets. A number of press reports suggest people thought they were safe here from the long arm of the law. In 1932, the licensee Samuel Simcock was fined £10 and £6 6s costs for allowing the upstairs smoke room of his hotel to be used by 'women of ill-repute'. Police witnesses stated they had seen half-naked women dancing round the floor, behaving in a suggestive manner, and heard them using offensive language. Simcock had been observed serving the women with alcohol on many occasions and had seen what was going on.

There were two instances which indicated the pub had been popular with American GIs. In June 1949, customs officials investigated the sale of American cigarettes to customers at the hotel. 11,000 cigarettes were found on the premises which licensee James Weston claimed had been left by US military personnel. A label on the cartons containing the cigarettes read 'For the use of US Forces only'. Weston said the cigarettes had been sold without his knowledge or authority but was fined £130 by the magistrates' court. The following October, Weston was in court again, charged with harbouring 331 pairs of American nylons. He said they had been left by an un-named American soldier, and was fined a further £500.

The Fatted Calf became known world-wide when it featured in the 1960 film 'Hell Is a City'. In the crime thriller, it is known as 'The Lacy Arms' although the interior may have been filmed at Elstree Studios. Some were offended that Manchester was being branded as 'Hell' and indignantly suggested that Hammer Films should shoot it elsewhere. The film's producer had to explain that the title came from a quotation by English poet Percy Shelley (1792-1822) and referred to London:

'Hell is a city much like London -
A populous and a smoky city;
There are all sorts of people undone,
And there is little or no fun done;
Small justice shown, and still less pity'.

Filmed in black and white, there were glimpses of other parts of Manchester's 'Lost District' in the

A map of Manchester made some time between 1650 and 1673 indicated the site of the cockpit (B) from a passage leading off Market Place. (E) was the Meal House.

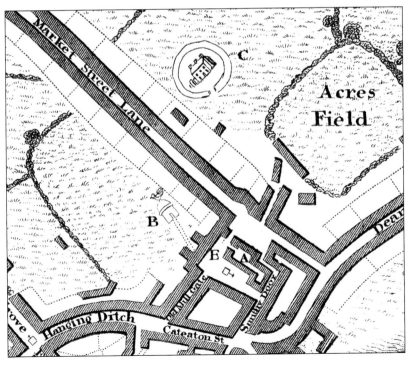

film: Cockpit Hill which had been re-named Higgitt's Passage, Cromford Court, Cannon Street, Corporation Street and Sefton's pub all feature. The film had its world premiere at the Ardwick Apollo. It has been suggested that although it was a well-made British film of the period, its greatest strength was the depictions of the locations shot around Manchester and Oldham.

People remembered the Fatted Calf's quaint reading room with its brass paper racks. In 1961 the pub was threatened with closure following the purchase of the property by the tailors, Montague Burton. Ken Malkin, a barman who had worked there, said that the 'Fatted' could be a hectic place in the evenings with its regular characters. Some called it the 'Strangeways Pop' because they would pop in there for their last pint before being picked up by the police. Then, after being released from Strangeways, they would pop in for a first pint.

The Fatted Calf and, to the left, Pie Entry 1910.

James Patrick's Correct Cards

Patrick, a letter-press and copper-plate printer, moved from Market Street to offices at 6 Cockpit Hill. He mainly printed material associated with horse racing - lists with the names, weights and colours of the riders, and the finishing lists of races. At the time of the big races, crowds would gather outside the Fatted Calf to get the official details. He would distribute his printed lists across Manchester via sellers who would rush around the streets shouting 'Patrick's krekt Card' in the mornings, then 'Patrick's full return list' in the evening. John Harnet, one of Patrick's 'criers' stood with the lists for many years by the Pie Entry in Market Street. He was well-known locally and often sketched by visiting artists. Newspapers reported his death in 1843 aged 92.

Patrick also sold the annual Pocket Racing Calendar of all the year's races. The Courier newspaper described the scene at Kersal Races in June 1841. There was an atmosphere of bustle and excitement as the vendors of Patrick's Correct cards mingled with ballad singers, stable grooms dressed in corduroys and white jackets, and stall-holders tempting the public with three goes for a penny. Patrick died aged 44 in 1837 but the business was continued for over twenty years by his brother Joseph.

STUDD'S LONDON CHOP-HOUSE

Chop-houses began in London in the 1690s where they served portions of meat known as chops. They came to Manchester in 1824 with the opening of the London Beef Steak and Chop-House in Fountain Street. Chops, steaks and soups were cooked entirely in the 'London style' and they supplied their French and English dishes to all parts of Manchester.

Today's Sam's and Thomas's (recently re-named Mrs Sarah's) Manchester chop-houses have their origins in Cockpit Hill. Thomas's London Chophouse was opened in 1866 by brothers Thomas and Samuel Studd, in a warehouse behind the omnibus office at 31 Market Street. They were from Bethnal Green in London, and Thomas had been a cook at Brown's London Chop-house for over ten years (See Sefton's, Corporation Street). Then in 1867 the brothers dissolved the partnership, with Thomas leaving to open his own chop and sandwich rooms on Cross Street.

The following year Samuel changed the Cockpit Hill business to his name. He moved to 44 Market Street in 1872 and was granted a drinks licence for the 1500 people who dined there weekly, attended by 16 waiters. The old premises on Cockpit Hill were later pulled down.

Samuel Studd became a director of Milner's Safe Company, and also Dandicolle and Gaudin, producers of wines and spirits. At the Market Street business, he went into partnership with his brother John who became the licensee. The partnership was dissolved in 1892, but Samuel remained a director of Milner's for over forty years. He moved to Upper Norwood in London where he died at the age of 83 in 1927. In his will he stated his wish for a quiet, unostentatious burial, with no females to be invited to the funeral. This reflected the social attitudes of earlier times when publications such as 'Cassell's Household Guide' in 1878 advised women not to attend funerals because only women from the poorer classes were present at such occasions.

Samuel's elder brother, Thomas, with whom he had founded the Cockpit Hill chop-house, died aged 45 at Heaton Mersey in 1880. His wife Sarah took over the running of the chop-house as well as looking after their seven children .

Helen Webster

Cromford Court in the 1960s. It was described in 1911 as a 'straggling narrow byway ... with old houses where Scrooge might have dwelt and Marley's ghost could have ascended a broad staircase.'

CROMFORD COURT

Cromford Court was named after Richard Arkwright's mill at Cromford in Derbyshire. The Court formed the approach to a cotton twist warehouse he owned here in 1788. In the 1750s, this area was largely cottages and pigsties. Quincey and Duck's warehouse stood on the corner of Cromford Court. They were Irish linen importers and Quincey continued there until 1783. Quincey's son, Thomas de Quincey, was the author of the famous 1821 novel 'Confessions of an English Opium-Eater'.

Watchmen used to be employed to patrol the streets at night time, checking for fires. As they went on their rounds they would shout out the time and a brief description of the weather. They wore brown top coats and broad-rimmed hats with a yellow band. They were nicknamed 'Charleys' and stationed in wooden huts known as 'watch-boxes'. A watchman at Cromford Court sometimes found himself tipped out of his hut by unruly youths late at night.

CROMFORD HOUSE

The five-storey Cromford House with shops, 100 offices and billiard rooms, was completed in 1926 by Manchester architect Albert Winstanley who also designed theatres and cinemas. Eleanor Mitchell who worked there for a typewriter company was the quickest typist in Europe. She gave demonstrations at Cromford House in 1928, typing 900 characters a minute and, within an hour, an average of 130 words a minute. She never looked at the keyboard and could type blindfolded or have a conversation while working. Before she began typing words, she was able to type the alphabet backwards and forwards 21,000 times. Her talent was discovered while at school and she went on to win many typing contests where she would be tested with words such as 'anti-disestablishmentarians' and 'septuagenarian'.

Manchester Chess Club moved to Cromford House in 1936. They had been based at the Clarion Café in Manchester until its demolition. A large room in the basement which was part of the Rialto Café was partitioned off for their use. It was one of only two venues in the North West where chess was played daily, except Sundays. Manchester was noted for its underground cafés where chess and draughts could be played, and at lunch-times, the Rialto would have up to 80 games under way. It reached its peak before World War II, when many of the participants went to serve in the forces. In the early 1900s chess had been popular with women who had learned the game at Victorian young ladies' academies.

For the best Luncheons and Teas.
Cromford Café
and
Grill Room.
5, Cromford Court, Manchester
(off Market Street and Corporation Street).
Open All Day Sunday.

Above: 1922 advertisement.

Left: The Cromford Club was in the basement of Cromford House (See next page). A croupier who worked there remembered Matt Busby, Ken Barnes, Pat Phoenix and Alderman Leslie Lever being regular guests. Artistes including the Bachelors, Joseph Locke and Jean Blanchflower, singer wife of Manchester United footballer Jackie, performed there. It was the venue for Catholic and Jewish fund-raising dinners. Bookmakers used to conduct business using ticker tape machines for the runners and riders, and racing results.

Workmen looking for an electricity main in Cromford Court following road subsidence in February 1940 discovered a brick-arched passageway leading in the direction of the Cathedral. The long-forgotten underground route had collapsed and, sadly, no further investigations were made. In this view looking towards Corporation Street and M&S, Cromford House is just seen on the right-hand side.

In 1920, there had been Sugarman's Kosher restaurant in Cromford Court. Then from 1946 to 1953, the Hadassiah Jewish restaurant.

THE CROMFORD CLUB

The Cromford Club opened in 1954 under the management of Paddy McGrath, an ex-boxer. This was one of the city's first late-night cabaret venues with restaurant and dance floor. It proved very popular, and had 1300 members within a year of opening. Professional footballers were frequent visitors and the police held parties here. The Manchester City team are said to have celebrated here when they won the championship in 1968, with the rival United players also present.

Cromford House.

The Cromford Club was raided in the early hours by police in June 1963. There were about 250 in the club at the time when blackjack and roulette were being played. Amongst those summoned for illegal gaming were a city magistrate from Bowdon and his wife; singer Karl Denver, and a Salford police sergeant. It was also alleged that the premises were being used during afternoons as an unlicensed betting office. They and the others summoned were cleared of wrong-doing, except five croupiers who were each fined £10. Years before in 1927, the owner of an office at Cromford House was fined £20 and £5 costs for allowing his premises to be used for betting purposes. The Cromford Club ceased to provide entertainment in 1969 in favour of gambling. When the area was redeveloped, the club moved to Canal Street to become the Playboy Club.

1849 OS map shows how Corporation Street cut through streets including Cockpit Hill.

1. Fatted Calf PH
2. Grotto PH
3. Malcolm Ross & Sons
4. Cromford House
5. Magic Village
6. Sefton's PH
7. Corporation Street
8. Market Street

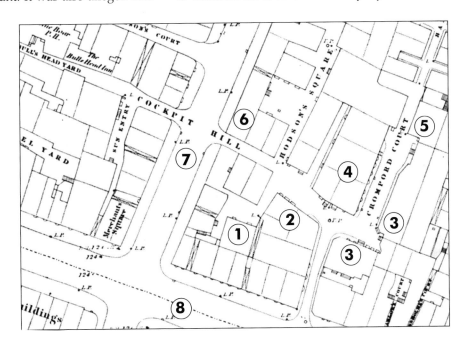

Keith Warrender

MAGIC VILLAGE

The Magic Village at 11 Cromford Court opened in March 1968 and was one of the many ventures of influential promoter, DJ and manager Roger Eagle. The Jigsaw Club and then the Cavern preceded the Magic Village which was advertised as a new scene for lovers of blues, West Coast and folk music. It was only open a few years but has achieved legendary status. Many famous bands played here including Pink Floyd, Jethro Tull and Fleetwood Mac. David Bowie was famously nearly refused admission because he was not recognised. Bowie played there before his show at the Free Trade Hall the following evening.

Eagle regarded the Magic Village as a 'psychedelic youth club' which promoted the progressive music of groups such as Captain Beefheart, John Mayall's Bluesbreakers and The Nice. It was situated in a damp cellar and there are several websites with memories of the club. People recall,

apart from the great bands, the 'all-nighters' from 11.30pm to 7am, the swirling dancers, and the light shows. People used to squat there in sleeping bags on benches and ledges.

Eagle was stocky, 6'4" and resembled American actor Tom Selleck. He was not good with finances and lived a bohemian existence in a converted coal cellar in Chorlton. He was a charismatic character who was dedicated to bringing new music to a wider audience and is also credited with pioneering Northern Soul - the music and dance movement. He was immensely knowledgeable on music and regarded as an educator. The Magic Village closed in January 1970, with Eagle possibly owing money, and moving back to Liverpool. He returned to Manchester in the early 1980s and set up the International Club. Later he moved to Llanfairfechan, North Wales, and died of cancer in 1999 aged 57.

Grotto pub - shaft discovery

The Grotto was in existence by 1882 when it was owned by William Wignall (See the Fatted Calf) whose business had gone into liquidation. He remained the owner until 1894 when it was auctioned. Its licence was withdrawn in 1903 because of non-residence. The following year while the building was being demolished, a 40ft-deep circular brick shaft was discovered.

There was a passage at the bottom which was said to extend beneath Market Street. The shaft was similar to the one found in premises at the corner of Cannon Street and New Brown Street in 1954 (See Wishing Well Café). A large number of old coins were also found at the Grotto during the demolition.

Malcolm Ross and Sons

The company were yarn-spinning manufacturers at 11 Cromford Court. The founder, Malcolm Ross (1811-1880), started at a firm in Glasgow at the age of ten. He became the Manchester representative of the company in 1832 and was made a partner. He formed his own company in 1834 and by 1837 had purchased premises in Cromford Court formerly belonging to Richard Arkwright, along with the looms already installed in the building. The company exported as far as China, Japan and India. Malcolm Ross was remembered for his huge mutton-chop whiskers, frock coat and stovepipe hat. He was president of the local Chamber of Commerce, and its treasurer for many years.

In civic life, along with Edward Watkin he was honorary secretary of the public parks committee, responsible for raising funds to acquire estates to be made into public parks. Through their and Mark Philips' efforts, Queen's Park, Philip's Park and Peel Park were opened in 1846. Ross cut the first sod in the conversion of the Hendham Hall Estate which became Queen's Park, a recreational space for public use. He promoted the work of the public library scheme, as well as the Mechanics' Institution. Ross also assisted Richard Cobden in the 1860 Paris Treaty and was on committees for

Ross Collection

Malcolm Ross

the welfare of ex-soldiers. Away from his business, civic and political duties he was a keen golfer and poet.

After his death in 1880 the company continued to be run by the family. Charles (1844-1930), one of his sons, later became the senior partner. He was born at Smedley Old Hall in Cheetham Hill and insisted there should be no female stenographers in the business as he was surrounded at home by four daughters along with four female domestic servants. Therefore employees had to write letters and reports by hand.

Charles Ross foresaw the importance of building the Manchester Ship Canal, and actively promoted the idea. He was a man of great vitality, and was a member of the Royal Exchange for 62 years and actively involved in the running of both the yarn business and two other cotton mills. He also regularly visited Liverpool to buy cotton, and on his return to his home in Wilmslow would either spend an hour sawing wood or go for a five-mile walk. He enjoyed travelling and was thought to be one of the first Englishmen to visit the French battlefields after the Franco-Prussian War. He claimed he knew Paris better than London.

Malcolm Ross & Sons, Cromford Court.

Amongst the yarn company's employees was George Berry who worked there for 70 years in the same department, under four generations of the Ross family, starting at the age of 14. He retired in 1946, also withdrawing from the Hallé Choir after 59 years' membership. He was also choirmaster at St Paul's, Withington. The company was then in the charge of cousins James and Oliver, great grandsons of the founder, and they vacated the premises about 1970. The company is now based in Alderley Edge although none of the Ross family are now involved.

Top right: The original oak staircase from Arkwright's premises.

Right opposite: Stickers attached to goods to identify the destination.

Below: Peter Ross, with his great-great-grandfather's accounts book from 1834.

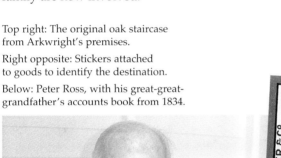

Joseph Hanson -
the Weaver's Friend

Hanson's Court was named after William Hanson, merchant and manufacturer of textiles, who lived and conducted his business here. In 1772 he was a check manufacturer. The 1800 directory lists him with his son Joseph, manufacturing silk and cotton handkerchiefs. Joseph worked in the business from the age of seventeen, receiving goods from Pendleton weavers where he lived. He would have known about their difficult working conditions and had a reputation for fairness.

Joseph was an enthusiastic supporter of King and country and involved in the leadership of the Volunteer Movement in Manchester as the country prepared to fight a possible invasion of Napoleon's troops. Earlier in 1782 the Volunteer Act was passed and Manchester sent 150 men to fight in the American War. By 1802, volunteering had waned and Colonel Hanson, who had moved to Strangeways Hall by 1807, was credited with reviving interest with the formation of the Loyal Masonic Volunteer Rifle Corps. They were known to have frequently used his grounds for drills and shooting practice.

In 1804, he commanded the Manchester, Salford, Bury and Stockport Rifle and Pikemen. Later that year he was arrested for taking part in a duel with Colonel Leigh Philips at Kersal Moor. They had quarrelled over who should lead the Manchester and Salford Volunteers which was an amalgamation of various militias. Hanson insisted on a duel despite Philips'

reluctance because he had a young family. Fortunately the men's friends called the police to intervene before the fight took place, and they were bound over to keep the peace. Hanson was later given command of the brigade but Leigh and over half the rank and file resigned in protest. As a result, another brigade was raised. Salford Museum have a glass goblet in their collection with the crest and monogram of Hanson, and the inscription 'Success to the Royal Manchester and Salford Volunteers of 1805'. There was growing national criticism of the Volunteers and in 1807 Hanson resigned his commission and devoted his

William Hanson's house and place of business.

Manchester Libraries, Information and Archives

energies to his political aspirations. He had realised that the militias were being used not only as a counter- invasion force but also to suppress protesting workers.

Hanson was concerned about the effects of war with France on the lives of working people. Wages were held down and trade with the United States had been closed, resulting in great hardship and misery. He instigated a 'Petition For Peace' which was signed by 40,000 people around the country. Also, after unsuccessful attempts in Chester and Stafford, he became a Parliamentary candidate in Preston for 'The Friends of Independence' political group in 1807. In his speeches he promised to uphold the rights of the Crown and the privileges of the people. During a meeting with weavers he gave his support to their campaign for guaranteed minimum wages. He narrowly lost against the two existing MPs, and denounced employers who had sacked workers because they had voted for him. Both his resignation from the military and his political views drew much criticism from contemporaries.

Hanson became known as the Weavers' Friend for his championing of the cause of the working man. The weavers sent a petition to Parliament in 1808 requesting minimum rates of pay to be fixed. This was a risky act, as workers were liable for prosecution if they organised petitions - only employers were allowed to appeal against working conditions.

Unsurprisingly, the vested interests of Westminster turned down the petition without a single voice in their favour. On hearing the bad news, some of the weavers met together on 22 May 1809. They and their families were starving and they had few options. As a result, about 600 weavers gathered the following day. They were urged by the Borough Reeve to disperse but remained even

after being read the Riot Act. The military were brought in at 1pm and the two sides faced each other until 4pm when the weavers left the field.

The weavers resented how they were being treated. They went on strike the next day and returned in much greater numbers to St George's Field, Rochdale Road (near the present Miller Street and Swan Street) where they were bolstered by workers from the outlying districts. Delegates were sent to negotiate with the local authorities but nothing was achieved. Again the Borough Reeve addressed the crowd, said to be over ten thousand, demanding they go back home, otherwise he would take action. The weavers refused to move and the 4th Dragoon Guards were brought in. But, as one of the weavers said, 'They may as well stay there and be killed, as go home and see their families starved!'.

As the situation grew more tense Joseph Hanson arrived in the afternoon on a white horse accompanied by his groom and rode through the crowd. He had been kept informed of events and had come to try to bring a peaceful end to the proceedings. He took off his hat and bowed to the crowd who began cheering him. It is unlikely most of them would have known who he was but he seemed to represent some sort of hope in the situation. Hanson asked the commanding officer if he could address the crowd but this was refused and he was ordered off the field. But as Hanson made his way through the crowd he began talking to them. He explained his own origins in weaving, and how he was their friend and supported them. He told them to carry on with their campaign but encouraged them to behave peacefully. The crowd started to cheer him which seems to have caused his horse to rear up and unseat him. He was next seen on his groom's horse riding home to Strangeways Hall. By 7pm the weavers had dispersed but not before an innocent bystander had been shot dead.

Guardian

Building in Hanson's Court with Arkwright associations, taken down in 1913.

carriage and drew it themselves. He held a rally at Ardwick Green at which people were encouraged to wear a sprig of evergreen, the emblem of reform which was later worn at Peterloo. Hanson was proud of his association with the weavers and his carriage had a shuttle emblem on both doors.

In 1811 he gave evidence to a Parliamentary Committee regarding the poor wages and working conditions of Manchester mechanics, spinners, weavers and calico printers. The effects of being in prison took its toll and he died later that year, aged 37, at Strangeways Hall. He was buried at Stand Unitarian Chapel, Whitefield. The family vault was said to have contained his portrait holding a shuttle, and an inscription that his efforts were a reminder to those in happier times of one who had loved his fellow man in darker days.

A building said to have been constructed by Sir Richard Arkwright was situated in Hanson's Court. It is not known what it was used for, but the many windows suggest it involved manufacturing. It was demolished in 1913.

While his actions may have seemed reckless and potentially inflammatory, Hanson's intervention probably saved a great deal of bloodshed on the day and was worthy of commendation. The following year, however, the authorities took a different view and he was arrested for taking part in the meeting, and charged with 'conspiracy to raise weavers' wages'. He was sentenced to six months' imprisonment at Lancaster and fined £100. In recognition of his efforts, weavers wanted to pay his fine with penny subscriptions which he graciously declined. Nevertheless, 39,600 people subscribed towards a gold cup and salver which were later presented to him, and a medal was produced in his honour.

After his release from prison, thousands lined the streets of Macclesfield, Stockport and Manchester to cheer him. Onlookers took the horses from his

Arkwright built the first steam-powered mill in Manchester at Miller Street, then known as Miller's Lane, in 1782. He had a cotton twist warehouse in Cromford Court, and in 1800 he was listed as a cotton spinner at 9 Cromford Court. By 1931, the refurbished part of the warehouse was the home of the Manchester Press Club.

Building mystery

Thomas Swindells, the Manchester historian, wrote about an old building in Hanson's Court which had an interesting window and was possibly used as a chapel. There are no records to confirm this, however excavations in the court some years previously revealed a substantial quantity of human remains.

Corporation Street looking towards Market Street in the 1960s.

CORPORATION STREET

As the name suggests, this was a scheme promoted by the Corporation. The street had been proposed by the Improvement Committee in 1843 and work commenced in 1845 to purchase and remove buildings on the line of the new thoroughfare.

This involved the demolition of old buildings around Cockpit Hill, Hodson's Court and Macdonald's Lane. The first 265-yard long section between Market Street and Todd Street was finished by August 1846. The second section up to Ducie Bridge was completed at a cost of over £47,000 and helped to relieve traffic congestion. It also provided an important link to the growing suburb of Cheetham Hill. Again, a great deal of dilapidated property was taken down to make way for the new road extension.

The newly-completed road, along with other streets, was used for unofficial omnibus races between the rival companies in November 1857. This drew large enthusiastic crowds but was of obvious concern to the city authorities.

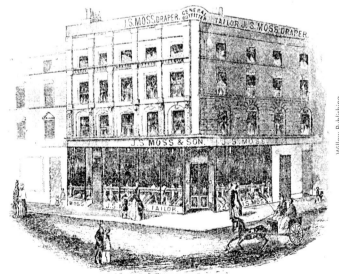

J S Moss and Son, tailors and drapers, were on the corner of Market Street and Corporation Street until the early 1900s, and according to their letterhead, they had been in business since the 17th century.

Manchester Libraries, Information and Archives

Sainsbury's Café, later Sefton's Public House, 12 & 14 Corporation Street.

SEFTON'S BAR

Sefton's quick-lunch bar and smoke-rooms opened in 1924. Its exterior is seen in the 1960 film 'Hell is a City'. Later, the Sefton's site was incorporated into the Manchester Arndale and became known as The Samuel Pepys, then The Isaac Newton and finally Paddy's Rat & Carrot at the time of the IRA bomb in 1996. It was credited as being the first in the city with a video jukebox.

Francis and Arthur Dickson, seed merchants and nurserymen, moved to 14 Corporation Street in 1854 from Deansgate. Arthur was a magistrate and became Mayor of Chester in 1885.

Then in 1873, William and Mary Brown opened a chop-house at numbers 10 and 14. The Browns had previously run the Exchange Hotel and chop-house since about 1852 until the building of the new Exchange. In 1883, they advertised the day hotel with the chop-house on Corporation Street.

Possibly the earliest chop-house in Manchester was the London Beef Steak and Chop-House which opened in 1824 on Fountain Street.

Mary Brown continued to run the business after her husband's death until her retirement in 1896, when the restaurant was converted into Sainsbury's Cold Luncheon Bar. This was owned by the Anderson family who had other establishments at Exchange Street East and in Liverpool. It was reputedly a favoured stopping-off place for businessmen. In November 1913 a smartly dressed passer-by inexplicably smashed three of its windows with his walking stick causing £10 damage. He was chased by the police, arrested and taken to the magistrates' court. The man, identified as Walter Stamford, said his behaviour had been due to worry and illness while the prosecution believed he was drunk. The stipendiary magistrate sent him to prison.

The daring young man of Corporation Street

The stamp shop at 24 Corporation Street was owned by Dolph Ostara (1860-1918), a former internationally-known trapeze artist. Born in St Petersburg of German descent, he was performing gymnastic feats from the age of five. He came to this country in 1884 when he and his brother Charles began performing as The Ostaras. They toured the world with their act which was the first to feature being caught or hanging by the toes.

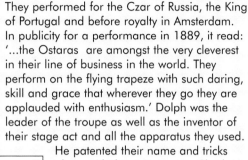

They performed for the Czar of Russia, the King of Portugal and before royalty in Amsterdam. In publicity for a performance in 1889, it read: '...the Ostaras are amongst the very cleverest in their line of business in the world. They perform on the flying trapeze with such daring, skill and grace that wherever they go they are applauded with enthusiasm.' Dolph was the leader of the troupe as well as the inventor of their stage act and all the apparatus they used. He patented their name and tricks along with the stage props. Charles later retired from the act and Dolph hired others in the troupe of three.

It was a hard profession to continue year after year with daily practices, and frequent knocks, and Dolph even performed with a partly dislocated knee. 'Miss Ostara' who was with the troupe in 1885, fell nine feet during one of the performances in Glasgow. A letter from the Ostaras to a newspaper gave assurances that the young lady was not too badly hurt and would soon return to the act.

Willow Publishing

During the time he was touring, Dolph continued to pursue his other interest of rare stamp dealing which he found profitable. After announcing his retirement from the trapeze troupe in 1895 he concentrated on his stamp business. He had a shop at 18 Piccadilly, Manchester and moved to Corporation Street about 1899. He tried to restrain a man in his shop in 1906 who had brought in stamps stolen from another dealer. In the ensuing struggle, Ostara fell through a glass partition and suffered cuts to his head, hands and back. The thief was shortly arrested in Market Street and Ostara made a full recovery. At the time of his death he and his family resided in Whalley Range.

MACDONALD'S LANE

Macdonald's Lane was in existence by 1764 when two houses were listed for auction at a yearly rent of £13 10s. By the 1830s, the area around Macdonald's Lane, along with Cockpit Hill and Pool Fold, formed the business heart of Manchester close to the Exchange.

Sir Elkanah Armitage, one of Manchester's best known merchants, had bed tick works at Macdonald's Lane and Cannon Street. 'Bed ticks' were mattress-sized bags filled with feathers or straw. Later he moved his works to Swinton and then Pendleton.

As Borough Reeve of Salford, he laid the first stone of the Victoria Bridge. He was elected as a councillor in Manchester and served for two years as Mayor. During his second term, he was involved in the quelling of local riots, and awarded a knighthood for his efforts in 1848. Armitage was a trustee of both the Grammar School and Royal Infirmary and also a JP and High Sheriff of Lancashire.

Brumme's, Macdonald's Lane.

BRUMME'S

Franz Frederic Brumme had one of the earliest delicatessens in the area at 11 Macdonald's Lane. In directories he was listed as a provision dealer, and also had a salmon smokery. Born in Brandenburg, Germany, in 1869, he had resided in Manchester since 1894 and became a British subject in 1911. Rates records in 1895 indicate he was in business at 23 Bridge Street before moving to Macdonald's Lane in 1908. He had begun his business with the help of a friend who lent him £5.

Ruth Pitt remembered being taken to Brumme's in 1938 when she was about five. Rickety wooden stairs led to a room with yellow lighting and a wonderful aroma. Brumme's was one of the few places outside London selling continental and overseas delicacies, and pioneers in the production of pre-prepared commercially made potato and vegetable salads.

During June 1937 Franz Brumme was a speaker at the Round Table Conference for World Peace at Cross Street Chapel. At the meeting, as the secretary of the German Club, he outlined his view that every nation hated war but found themselves involved through faulty economic systems.

In 1939, amidst growing antagonism towards Germany, as the Nazis rose to power, Brumme wrote a letter to the Manchester Evening News. He distanced himself from prominent Nazi sympathisers such as Carl Goedecke, who had a factory in Trafford Park, and Otto Baumbache, a glass instrument manufacturer who held meetings at the German Lutheran Church Hall in Greenheys. The social club was a meeting place for German nationals. Brumme stated that, as one of the church's lay leaders, he did not associate with them and had banned them from attending. After his death in 1954 in Poynton, a memorial service was held at St David's, Victoria Park. His son Franz Conrad took over the business.

HODSON'S SQUARE

The Hodson family were substantial landowners locally with Hodson's Court off Corporation Street, and Hodson's Square where William Hodson, a merchant, built three warehouses and offices in 1796. The properties in the Square along with those in nearby Kinder's Court were destroyed by fire in 1800. It had begun accidentally and caused over £50,000 of damage. In 1792 Hodson was president of the Manchester Church and King Club which was against Dissenters who tried to repeal the 1661 Corporation Act. Legislation barred anyone from membership of town corporations who would not adhere to the rites of the Church of England. The Act was eventually repealed in 1828.

The City Betting Club at 7 Hodson's Square, owned by Thomas Swarbrick, opened in 1884. He had other betting clubs in Brown Street and Sackville Street. They were unlicensed and had sprung up with many others around the city. The Mayor of Manchester described them as 'places of unlicensed wickedness'. Publicans complained they were losing their best customers to these clubs where they could gamble and drink freely. It was feared that many young men who had not previously gambled were being lured into trouble.

The authorities had been aware of the problem since 1881 but were unsure whether they could intervene in the activities at the 'social' clubs. In 1883 the Home Secretary confirmed that local magistrates had the power to shut them down.

On the afternoon of 20th May 1885, 23 of the most notorious clubs were raided by police. It had been planned with a high degree of secrecy with only three in the force knowing of the plan. They organised it for the day when all of Manchester's police force were present for the annual inspection at their various divisional headquarters. Then after the inspection, at the given telephone signal, they were ordered to simultaneously surround the clubs at 2pm when it was considered they would be at their busiest.

The operation involved about four hundred police personnel who rushed to the clubs, making sure no-one escaped through windows and back doors. The presence of so many police drew a lot of attention and excitement amongst ever-growing crowds following them as 200 people were apprehended and 185 arrested. There were some violent scuffles, but it was more peaceful at the City Club and ended quite quickly. There had been over a hundred present, and thirteen were arrested and marched through the streets to the Town Hall. Four bookmakers who were apprehended at the club were later fined £25 and five guineas added costs.

Swarbrick's clubs were closed and by 1886 he was declared insolvent. He was given a suspended discharge from bankruptcy in 1893. He had begun in business in 1873 with a tripe shop in Bolton, then later had shops in Manchester and Salford before opening his first betting club in 1882.

Barber's impropriety

The manageress of the lady barbers at 2 Macdonald's Lane was brought to court in 1916, charged with keeping a disorderly house. The premises also contained a café, shaving salon and manicure cubicles. Amy Morrison indignantly denied that the cups of tea, cigarettes and kissing and cuddling offered by her two attractive assistants, Mabel and Lily were untoward. The police alleged that impropriety took place when curtains were drawn across the cubicles. Morrison was fined £10 for keeping a disorderly house.

Kaiserman Collection

Cannon Street from the corner of Corporation Street. The western end of Cannon Street was widened in 1906 in line with the bank on the corner towards Cateaton Street.

Discovery in Cannon Street

There has been speculation about how the street got its name. It could have been named after the London street, as was the fashion in those times. The street in the capital was so named because of its residences of the Dean and Canons of St Stephen's Collegiate Chapel.

However a key piece of information about Manchester's Cannon Street was to be found in a 1918 auction catalogue. A sale of contents from Davenport Hall near Congleton included 'Lot 892 - Pair of old six-pounder iron cannon, mounted on carriages, which form an interesting relic of old Manchester ... which are said to have given rise to the naming of Cannon Street.' In another version of the catalogue they were described as a pair of 'Antique ornamental' cannon. At the auction conducted by Artingstall & Hind Ltd of Manchester on behalf of Colonel Robert Francis Gartside -Tipping, the cannon were sold for £8 10s to a Mr Banks of Congleton.

By 1764 Hunter's Lane was known as Cannon Street as Manchester expanded. In November 1874, during work to renew pavements on Cannon Street, two iron stumps were removed from the end of Back Tipping Street. As work progressed, it was discovered that the two stumps were the muzzles of two old cannon that had been buried upright. They were about seven ft long with a two-and-a-half inch bore. One of them had markings 'N.V.2-0-4' near the touch hole. So it would seem that many in Manchester had known about the cannon at the side of the thoroughfare extending from Hunter's Croft.

The cannon were thought to belong to the Tipping family, who were the current owners of property at Back Tipping Street. The two guns were said to have stood either side of Tipping's Court. There was a school for poor children within the court in 1711 paid for out of the rents of other properties as stipulated in the will of Catherine

108

Richards which also provided for merchants' widows. Within the vicinity was also Tipping Street and Little Tipping Street. In 1800, Thomas Tipping and Company were manufacturers and calico printers at 1 Tippings Court, along with Tipping and Walker, yarn and cotton merchants, at number 9. The cannon came from one of the family's trading ships and were thought to have been later placed outside their private residence. The Tipping family had requested that the cannon should be returned to them, and the guns remained in their possession until the 1918 auction.

What happened to the cannon next, remains a mystery. The identity of the buyer is not clear, and the auctioneers are now based in California. No-one in Congleton seems to know of the cannon's whereabouts. It is quite possible the cannon were melted down for the war effort.

Lt-Col. Tipping's country seat was Rossferry House, County Fermanagh.

The 1746 Casson and Berry map of Manchester shows open fields and gardens beyond Hunter's Lane stretching towards the houses in Marsden Square and High Street, and yet more open space going eastwards to Shudehill. When Cannon Street was constructed in the 1760s, it was originally a residential area, but by the nineteenth century it had become a centre for the textile trade. The residents had moved out to the suburbs and the street was lined with warehouses and other commercial premises. In the 1840s, people could still remember earlier times when partridges used to be shot in the Cannon Street district.

In 1930 there were further proposals to widen Cannon Street in order to ease the traffic

The Tipping Family

The family can be traced back to 1566 in the Manchester Court Leet Records, after Richard Tipping moved from Preston to live at a mansion later named Tipping Gates near the Collegiate Church. Tippings had held the important role of Borough Reeve in the 1750s and 1760s. Tipping's Court had been in existence since about 1778 with a John Tipping living there amongst the warehouses.

After the death of Joseph Tipping in 1800 at Crumpsall it was written that 'the loss of this worthy man would be felt by family, friends and the poor'. Thomas Tipping, who died in 1846, had been Lord of the Manor of Bolton and lived at Davenport Hall. It was his grandson who sold the cannon.

Another Thomas, the merchant who had his business at Tipping's Court, lived with his wife and nine children in Ardwick where he also

owned several pieces of land. A street was also named after him. At his death in 1815 the business closed, but his wife Ann continued to live in Ardwick until her death in 1833.

Henry, the son of Gartside Tipping, entered the Navy in 1860, then after his retirement he became Inspector of Lifeboats on the Irish and west of England coasts. He was also involved in the Missions to Seamen. At the outbreak of World War I he re-enlisted and was given command of a ship. He was then in his 60s, and said to be the oldest officer in the Navy when he was killed in action off the Belgian coast in 1915, after his yacht 'Sanda' was sunk by gunfire. His wife died while serving in the Women's Emergency Corps in France two years later.

To be LEFT,
A HOUSE, in Tipping's Court,
MANCHESTER,
In the Possession of Mr. JOHN TIPPING,
With a Warehouse, Dye-House, Stove, &c.
Suitable for a SMALLWARE MANUFACTURER.
Enquire of Mr. Tipping.

Manchester Mercury 1779.

congestion along Market Street. It involved widening the stretch of Cannon Street between Back Tipping Street and Falcon Street in line with the London City and Midland Bank at the Corporation Street end, and Thomas Collier's premises on the corner of High Street. There were plans to line the new 74-feet wide thoroughfare with 'handsome shops and offices'.

Planners envisaged it as Manchester's Regent Street with well-designed and uniform architecture. However these expectations were dampened by another council official who stated 'The Corporation is not a body of house or shop builders...The land will come into our hands and all we shall do is let it.' Buildings were purchased for demolition at a cost of £200,000, but it was hoped the sale of building plots would raise £90,000.

The site of the former Independent Chapel, was included in the demolition area. (See page 152). The street never became a major shopping area, and because of severe financial restrictions, it took until 1943 to complete the road widening, with the remaining empty plots of land used as car parks.

Left: Car park Cannon Street 1969.

110

William Briggs and Co.

William Briggs (1845-1922) born in Blackley, had an imposing tile-covered works at 34 Cannon Street. He supplied goods for needlecraft under the 'Penelope' brand name. His shop, 'Mrs Bidders', at 5 St Ann's Passage sold his range of products including needlework transfers and kits. In the 1880s his works were on the north side of Cannon Street but had moved to the new building by 1917. He had been a woollen sales-man in 1871 and began his business in 1874.

He was a JP, chairman of the Mercantile Bank, and chairman of the Neptune Steam Navigation Company which ran a liner service between Baltimore and Rotterdam. His brother Thomas had been Mayor of Manchester. The company, in connection with the Coats Group, published the two journals Needlewoman and Needlecraft and other instructional publications issued from his premises on Cannon Street. During the last world war they provided embroidery kits to members of the forces in hospital or in isolated situations as a form of occupational therapy.

In 1912 Briggs presented his house - Bank Hall and the 15 acre estate at Heaton Mersey to the City of Manchester to be used as a home for neglected girls. At the time of his death he was living in Hale, just days after learning of the death of his second son.

Below: The corner of Corporation St and Cannon St c1897. Arthur Foote, whose shop on Corporation Street is seen on the right, was born in Cambridgeshire, and established his typewriter and stationery business in 1880. He later moved to Brown Street opposite the main post office. He lived in Higher Broughton and was a churchwarden at St Matthias, Salford. He took part in around 70 Whit Walks before his death in 1946.

The Courier newspaper

The newspaper was founded by Thomas Sowler (1789-1857) in 1825 at offices in St Ann's Square, in opposition to the Liberal Manchester Guardian. It began under the patronage of Sir Robert Peel, with the poet Alaric A Watts as its first editor. Sowler was a letterpress printer, then bookseller, before becoming a newspaper publisher and general printer. The family traced their ancestry back to Baron Sowler of Normandy. Thomas and his son narrowly escaped being sent to prison in a dispute with Jeremiah Garnett of the Manchester Guardian (See 'Manchester Guardian').

In 1831 the Courier sold 2,635 copies, whereas its main rival the Guardian sold 5,144. The Conservative-supporting paper was published on Saturdays until it became a four-page 'daily' in 1864. After Sowler's death, his sons Thomas and John took over the running of the paper. They moved to new purpose-built premises at 22 Cannon Street in 1878.

At the ceremony to lay the foundation stone, Thomas Sowler placed a bottle containing a copy of the first edition of the newspaper along with that day's edition and a list of all the employees into a cavity. In 1874 the company had introduced the Evening Mail but it was not a success.

Thomas, born in Bowdon in 1818 and educated at Manchester Grammar School, was knighted in 1890. He was an honorary Colonel of the 7th Manchester Volunteer Artillery, a JP and President of the National Association of Journalists. He was chairman of various Manchester Conservative organisations and a director of a number of companies. When he died in 1891 aged seventy three, the rival newspaper, the Guardian, was generous in its tribute to him. It said he had been a prominent figure in the political and commercial life of Manchester for fifty years. His eldest son, Thomas, became managing director until his death in 1899.

By this time the Sowler newspapers were experiencing financial problems. The Evening Mail closed in 1902 and the Courier was purchased in 1904 by Alfred Harmsworth who later became Lord Northcliffe. The paper ceased publication in 1916 for the duration of the war, but was never printed again.

Inset top: Sir Thomas Sowler 1818-1891.
Above: Nicol Dunn, editor 1905-1911.
Left: Going to press 1901.

Willow Publishing

Keith Warrender

The Play-Inn on the corner of Cannon Street and Lower Cannon Street 1969.

NEW BROWN STREET

The site on the corner of Market Street was bombed during WWII and work began in 1951 on a six-storey building. It was sited on the new Market Street building line, which was set back from existing businesses. William Timpson Ltd moved in after their shoe shop on Market Street had been destroyed, along with Price's tailors in 'temporary' single-storey shop units which lined up with the present buildings.

New Brown Street was known as the 'Carnaby Street' of Manchester because of the number of clothes shops there. They included at various times Serene, She Boutique, Jeffrey's Boutique and Clobber's Boutique. It used to attract crowds of teenagers on Saturdays, and Alex Britton, the owner of the Baked Potato Snack bar, had to employ a doorman to keep order. Bobby McDermot (See page 38) held a daily 9am meeting at the snack bar to organise his street vending business, as well as occasional meetings with the smartly-dressed Kray brothers. Bill Benny (See page 29) would come in at lunch times for a double meal. The Eighth Day was above Britton's café, and Ivor

Keith Warrender

Shop on the corner of Market Street and New Brown Street.

Hazan, founder of the 'Stolen From Ivor' stores, had a shop in the former Watts' theatrical costumier warehouse. Gerry Cohen also had a clothing shop in the street.

New Brown Street was originally the site of Tarr's Court with William and Thomas Tarr, fustian shearers and cutters, there in 1788. The rates records indicate William Tarr living in the court until 1817. A Sunday School was held in the street in 1786 with 60 boys and 30 girls, presumably from the nearby Independent Chapel on Cannon Street.

The new road between Market Street and Cannon Street to replace Tarr's Court was proposed in 1830 at a Ley-payer's meeting at the Town Hall. The line of Tarr's Court was extended by the purchase of four plots of land at a cost of £8,500. The town benefited from the renting of properties on either side of the new thoroughfare. In 1831, three cottages and an engine house were for sale in Tarr's Court. New Brown Street was in use by September 1833.

Boutiques on New Brown Street and signs for the Wishing Well Restaurant.

Manchester Libraries, Information and Archives

WISHING WELL RESTAURANT

The basement restaurant on the corner of New Brown Street and Cannon Street was originally known as the City Restaurant but was re-named in 1954 following the discovery of a deep shaft. The owner, Alex Britton, made it a feature by constructing an imitation wishing well into which people would throw coins. Before the restaurant's closure, the shaft was excavated down to about eighty feet. A chamber off the shaft, part way down, contained what may have been a coal storage area. Work on the shaft had to stop after three months with the developers of the Arndale site moving in.

Alex Britton with coins recovered from the well.

The restaurant was a popular late-night venue when there were few other places open at that time in the city. At weekends there was also a disco. One diner remembered getting into conversation with two young Liverpudlian men there. As they chatted about their respective families she found she had two things in common with one of them: they shared the same birthday and they both had a son named Julian. She later realised she had been talking to John Lennon and Paul McCartney!

People involved in the management of the construction of Guardian, the top secret underground communications network in Manchester, used to come to the Wishing Well in the late evening. In one of the quieter areas of the restaurant, they held discussions with large plans spread over the tables.

Tavern and consulate

The tavern at 22 Cannon Street was listed in the 1779 Manchester directory. It was the venue for a bankruptcy hearing in 1792. There was a well-attended meeting here in 1796 to form an association of proprietors to protect their warehouses from night theft. They proposed employing people to patrol the streets in the district between 8pm and 6am. Around that period there used to be only fifty-five watchmen employed by the town, which was insufficient. In 1881 the tavern's licence was opposed by the police because the tenant was not the actual residential occupier.

By 1930, 22 Cannon Street had become the office of the Finnish Consulate. In 1940 it was accepting applications from Britons to fight with Finnish forces against the invading Soviets.

Keith Warrender

Passage towards Cannon Street 1969.

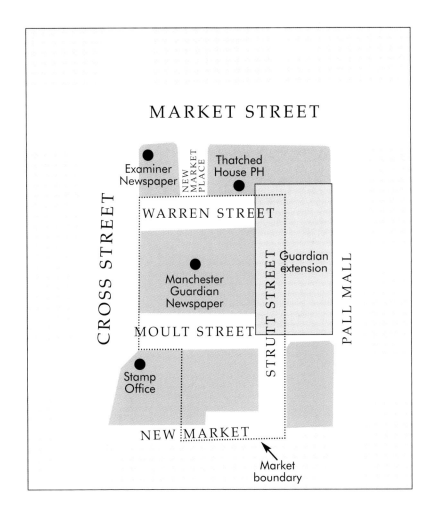

SECTION 3

MANCHESTER EXAMINER

Manchester Libraries, Information and Archives

The former Examiner offices on the corner of Market Street and Cross Street.

Text Society for his essay 'The City and the Shame of Britain'. He then won a writing competition organised by the National Anti-Corn Law League in 1854 which brought him to the attention of John Bright, Richard Cobden and Alexander Ireland who suggested he wrote for the Examiner.

He became editor in 1854 and continued until 1889. Whether he was writing about political controversies or more general topics his brilliance shone through. He was known to many through his newspaper articles written under the nom de plume of 'Verax'. It was said of him 'Few journalists of his time wielded a more vigorous or polished pen'. The Examiner reached its peak under his editorship; however he did not come out as strongly as the Manchester Guardian on the question of Irish Home Rule which lost readers to its rival. Also, some of Dunckley's colleagues did not appreciate his frequently leaving the offices early while they were still working on incoming news items. After his retirement he continued to write, before suddenly collapsing and dying on a tram in Oxford Road, Manchester.

According to Joseph Adshead's 1851 map, the Manchester Examiner occupied about a third of the space of the block known as the Examiner Offices on the corner of Market Street and Cross Street. The newspaper was established on 10th January 1846 to promote Liberal and Free Trade principles, backed by John Bright MP, and Edward Watkin MP and railway pioneer.

For the first few months, the offices were at Pall Mall, but later that year, they moved to newly-built offices at 22 Market Street. It began as a weekly paper, printed at 7 Pall Mall, then in July the following year it was published twice-weekly. The Manchester Times amalgamated with it in 1848.

HENRY DUNCKLEY

The Manchester Examiner was run in 1854 by Henry Dunckley and Alexander Ireland. Dunckley (1823-1896), born in Warwick became the pastor of Great George Street Chapel, Salford, where his preaching drew large congregations. His great promise as a writer was seen in 1849 after he won a prize awarded by the Religious

ALEXANDER IRELAND

Alexander Ireland (1810-1894) was associated with the Manchester Examiner for forty years as publisher and business manager. He joined as joint publisher in 1847, and during that period it became one of the most influential newspapers in the North of England. Ireland was the friend of many famous literary men of his time and was instrumental in bringing them and other notable speakers to the city.

He took an active part in the founding and running of the Manchester Free Library and assembled bibliographies of leading literary figures William Hazlitt and Leigh Hunt. He wrote and published biographies of his friend the great American writer, poet and philosopher Ralph Waldo Emerson, and also compiled the popular 'Book Lover's Enchiridion [Handbook]'. Ireland left the Examiner in 1888 when it was bought by the Manchester Press Company who invested £70,000 in its development. It was not a success and was sold again in 1891 to a syndicate led by Thomas Sowler, the owner of the Manchester Courier. The Liberal newspaper was in the difficult position of being run by a Tory owner, but it retained its political stance with the news and other articles coming from the Courier office. Finally in 1894, the Manchester Examiner became part of the Empire News.

Archibald Prentice - reformer

The Times's editor, Archibald Prentice (1792-1857), came to Manchester from Lanarkshire and spent the rest of his life pressing for social and political reform. He established the Manchester Times in 1828 and remained there until 1847. He influenced the views of many Manchester politicians and was not afraid to speak the truth as he saw it.

Prentice worked for a muslin manufacturer in Glasgow who transferred his business to a Manchester warehouse on Peel Street in 1815. He is said to have devoted his days to business and his evenings to politics. Through John Edward Taylor and others he became friends with 'the little circle', a group dedicated to liberal principles. This was the era when reformers were denounced as 'Jacobins', and many public houses had signs reading 'No Jacobins allowed here'. To be a reformer invited personal abuse and violence. The popular slogan then was 'Church and King, and down with the rump!' Prentice alerted the public to the Government's extensive system of spying with his article 'Beware of Spies' in 1817.

Prentice was a witness for John Edward Taylor, the founder of the Manchester Guardian, at his trial for criminal libel in Lancaster in 1819. He belonged to a group who thought that the Manchester Guardian did not go far or fast enough in their promotion of liberal principles, and was helped in the purchase of Cowdroy's Gazette in 1824. The newspaper got into financial difficulties and merged with the newly established Manchester Times in 1828.

He addressed a crowd of 6000 unemployed people in 1826. Other speakers had encouraged a riotous atmosphere but he managed to persuade about half of the workers to go home peacefully. However the next day there was a riot. Prentice addressed various meetings in Manchester and Salford to promote Parliamentary reform. He was one of the founders of the Manchester Anti-Corn-Law Association and frequently wrote and spoke on the subject.

He also firmly denounced slavery and the slave trade, and supported more education for the young, including Sunday Schools. Following the closure of public footpaths in Flixton he led the formation of the Manchester Association for the Protection of Ancient Footpaths, as well as campaigning for the removal of tolls on public bridges. The temperance movement also had his active support.

Prentice produced pamphlets on many of the issues he was passionate about. He also wrote 'Historical Sketches and Personal Recollections of Manchester and Salford' in 1851 which reflected the change in public opinion from 1792 to 1832, and then his 'History of the Anti-Corn Law League' in 1853. In his declining years in recognition of his efforts, he was awarded, through public subscription, an annuity of £100 for life and given a modestly-paid job with the gas office of Manchester Corporation.

He lived to see many of the things he had zealously fought for come into being, including Catholic emancipation, abolition of slavery, parliamentary and municipal reform, the adoption of penny postage and the repeal of the Corn Laws.

NEW MARKET

Most of the area in this section was covered by the site of the New Market. Because of overcrowding at Old Market Place, it was proposed in a meeting at the Bull's Head in 1775, to purchase plots of land known as Hyde Park and Pool Fold (later to become Cross Street) to build a new market close to the centre of Manchester. Land was purchased by Thomas Chadwick and Holland Ackers for a market hall and 144 open stalls. It opened in 1781 and was also referred to as the New Shambles.

The market hall site is marked by the present-day street 'New Market', and was situated at the eastern half of the street. The upper storey, used as a warehouse, was damaged by a fire in January 1786. The blaze had been accidentally started by a young employee who had tried to carry burning embers from one stove to light another. Two men were badly hurt during the fire.

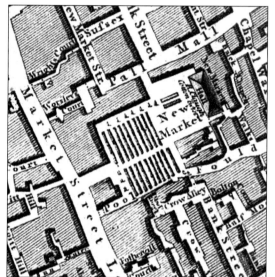

New Market on Laurent's 1793 map.

One fell from the second storey and another was injured when a beam gave way.

The hall had been restored sufficiently by the following June to hold an exhibition of Thomas Jervais's stained-glass pictures in the 'Great Room'. This was a large hall on the ground floor paved with flag stones, and vaulted below. Jervais was from Dublin and his work was to be found in castles, chapels, colleges and mansions. The Lower Swan Inn also exhibited his work on two occasions before his death in 1799.

The New Market closed in 1803 because it infringed the rights of the Lord of the Manor, Sir John Parker Mosley, who had not given permission for the extension to the old market. A new market had been built at the corner of Deansgate and Bridge Street by 1803. The old market site was sold to Mosley and the land built on.

Pool Fold and Radcliffe Hall

The name of Pool Fold derives from the name of the approach to Radcliffe Hall where there was a ducking stool next to a pool. By 1590 William Radclyffe had a 'cucking stool' on his land which was used to punish scolding wives and 'lewd-women'. Around 1602, after the pool had been filled in, the ducking stool was moved to one of the pits known as the Daub Holes in what is now Piccadilly. William's son, Captain Radcliffe, was the commander of the troops defending Market Stead Lane when Royalist forces besieged Manchester in 1642. He later became a member of Parliament. Radcliffe Hall was surrounded by a circular moat which was filled in about 1672. The hall was converted into the Sun Tavern and the King's Arms to serve customers at the New Market. The original Cross Street Chapel was later built close to the site of the pool next to Radcliffe Hall. The old thoroughfare, Back Pool Fold, still exists.

THATCHED HOUSE HOTEL

It was licensed in 1743, at 28 Newmarket Place but existed in 1623, when it was used as part of a network of selected inns for royal postal routes. The nearby Bull's Head was also used for this purpose in 1625. By 1790 Manchester was the biggest handler of mail outside London.

As the name suggests, it was originally a thatched house. A drawing made in 1822 indicates it had unusually tall chimneys which both helped to take the smoke away from the site and lessened the danger of sparks on the thatched roof.

A man who was gifted in making rhymes is said to have run up a large bill at the Thatched House which he couldn't pay. He got the inn-keeper to agree to his paying off his debts with some lines of verse for the new inn sign, which read:

'The farmer 'neath thatch keeps his stacks fro' the raine,
For elsewise would perish his hay and his graine:
But here we see men (what a contrary set)
Come under the thatch when they wish to get wet.'

The landlord was not impressed with the man's poetry and forcibly ejected him from the pub.

When the Thatched House was auctioned in 1822, there was a covenant within the agreement to rebuild, presumably during the Market Street widening scheme. It seems to have been pulled down and rebuilt in 1824 at a cost of £464. A Royal Exchange Assurance advertisement in that year directed customers to their office adjoining the 'new inn called the Thatched House Tavern'.

In 1828, the 'Jolly Tar' coach used to set off from here to Southport, and the 'Accommodation' departed for Dunham and Bolton. A coach office opened here in 1838 for services to neighbouring towns and Yorkshire and Lincolnshire. In January 1838 there was a meeting here to campaign for municipal reform. They wanted the chief officers to be elected by the townspeople, rather than

The hotel in 1970.

being nominated by jurors of the Lord of the Manor's Court Leet. That year Manchester was granted a Charter of Incorporation which began the process of reforming the Corporation. It took until 1846 with the purchase of the manorial rights to fully integrate Manchester's local authority powers.

The inn was a noted gathering place for tradesmen and country manufacturers in town for business. Many property auctions took place here. When the Tavern was being auctioned in 1842, it was described as having twenty-one beds and that it was frequented by many Irish and Scots buyers. The proprietor in 1865, William Whitterton, tragically died after being thrown from his gig while travelling one evening from Barlow Moor to Manchester. He was well-known in the sporting world and in 1864 had the best sow at the Worsley and Swinton Agricultural Show.

A new underground restaurant was built at the Thatched House in 1881 called 'The Dive', to attract city workers, including employees from the Manchester Guardian offices opposite. In the 1950s it was known as a jazz venue.

The Stamp Office

Stamps were sold there as well as deeds, leases and other legal documents which needed to be stamped. The office moved in 1847 from Newall's Buildings on the corner of Cross Street and Market Street to the new premises on the corner of Moult Street and Cross Street. Stamps were sold on the ground floor and the newspaper stamping office was in the basement. All published literature was taxed, with newspapers paying one penny tax per copy. Newspaper stamp duty was abolished in 1855.

There were two robberies at the Moult Street offices, the first in 1855 when coins and stamps worth an estimated £1,700 were stolen after thieves concealed themselves in the premises overnight. Two men were charged but released through lack of evidence.

In the second robbery in 1866, £10,000 of stamps were stolen. Four men were arrested and received sentences totalling 53 years. A few months later the convicted men confessed where they had hidden most of the stolen goods. As a result, £8000-worth of stamps were recovered from the luggage compartments at two London railway stations where the criminals were in the habit of stashing their ill-gotten gains.

The Stamp Office moved to Mount Street in 1874.

THE MANCHESTER GUARDIAN

The newspaper began in 1821 at 29 Market Street, below a cutler's shop, near the corner of New Cannon Street. The first edition was published on the 5th of May - the day of Napoleon's death. Between 1825 and 1828, following a merger with another newspaper, it was known as 'The Manchester Guardian and British Volunteer'. It ran as a weekly paper each Saturday until 1836 when a Wednesday edition was published. The paper moved to offices on Warren Street, off Cross Street, in 1841. The following year the newspaper expanded in size to be printed on double sheets. It became a 'daily' in 1855 following the abolition of stamp duty on newspapers.

The Manchester Guardian was founded and edited by John Edward Taylor with his business partner Jeremiah Garnett, a printer, publisher and reporter. They had decided to begin the newspaper to promote liberal ideas in response to the brutal 1819 Peterloo Massacre in Manchester, in which an estimated eighteen people died and about seven hundred were injured. Taylor along with another journalist, had sent detailed accounts to London newspapers of the military driving their horses into the crowd at the fateful demonstration, before the authorities put out the 'official' version.

Entry to Pool Fold and the Guardian offices off Market Street.

122

Left: The Manchester Guardian building in 1881 at 4 Warren Street.

Opposite page: The gateway entrance into Pool Fold, later Cross Street. The building was associated with John Hopps who had a circulating library and bookshop and regularly took extended summer holidays in the country-side. On another occasion when he was ill, he put up the shutters again, leaving a much-quoted notice in rhyme that he would return when he was better. In 1800 he was listed at 14 New Market, but earlier had been at 56 Bridge Street. Hopps was a tall man - 6ft 3in and generally enjoyed good health. He died in 1822 age 83 and was buried in Flixton. The book business continued to be run by his family.

In the prospectus for the forthcoming newspaper the owner stated the paper would 'zealously enforce the principles of civil and religious liberty', 'warmly advocate the cause of Reform', 'endeavour not to degenerate into calumny and abuse', and 'pay particular attention to all aspects of local interest'.

Before Jeremiah Garnett became editor, he and Thomas Sowler, the editor of the rival paper 'The Courier', made increasingly bitter accusations against each other in print in 1840. Sowler called Garnett 'an impudent and wilful perverter of the truth' and Garnett responded that the accusation was 'a crawling and cowardly lie'. Word reached Garnett that Sowler was looking for him, so Garnett set off to his offices in St Ann's Square to confront him. Sowler and his son came running to him and held his wrist while they tried to beat him with a small horsewhip. However, the burly Garnett got the better of his assailants and struck out with his umbrella. Passers-by intervened to stop the scuffle, and no-one was seriously hurt.

Sowler and son Robert were later summoned for assault. In court they were found guilty and sentenced to three months' imprison-ment. However they were saved by the petitions of Garnett and other influential friends who persuaded the judge to remit the sentence and they were fined just one shilling and bound over to keep the peace.

Jeremiah Garnett, editor 1844-1861.

John Edward Taylor, editor 1821-1844.

The Manchester Guardian building (right) designed by Barker and Ellis on Cross Street opposite the Royal Exchange.

A new Guardian building on the site was completed by 1886. It had the latest printing and typesetting machinery and electric lighting. Architecturally, it had its critics. Professor Charles Reilly described the gothic building in 1924 as not worthy of a newspaper which fostered art and architecture. He said it was a building of outdated conflicting styles and of 'warehouse coarseness' and hoped the Guardian would replace it with something more appropriate at the earliest opportunity and set a standard worthy of Cross Street and the whole of Manchester.

In 1928 work began on a rear extension designed by Harry S Fairhurst, over Strutt Street. The building replaced the 'Examiner and Times' newspaper offices which had been published there since 1846. The new building which fronted onto Pall Mall, was also the offices for the Manchester Evening News and City News. Foundations went down over forty feet to accommodate the print machinery.

The newspaper changed its name in 1959 to 'The Guardian' to reflect its wider significance. It closed its offices in 1970 with the site being required for the Arndale development. The editorial team had moved to Gray's Inn Road, London, six years previously. The closure of the Cross Street premises brought to an end almost 130 years of the Guardian on the site. Some of the staff moved to offices near Deansgate.

The offices in new extension on Pall Mall were completed by 1930.

CP SCOTT

Charles Prestwich Scott was editor of the Manchester Guardian between 1872 and 1929. He was the nephew of the founder John Edward Taylor. It was during his time as editor that the newspaper rose to national prominence with its liberal, progressive values. His paper backed the 1889 dockers' strike, the miners in 1893 and the engineers in 1897. It opposed the Boer War describing it as 'a shameful Imperialist adventure'. The Guardian played a key part in the Liberals coming to power in 1906 and also supported women's suffrage and Irish Home Rule.

Scott encouraged his journalists to write in plain English. He saw it as his mission to make issues clear to ordinary people, and disliked the pedantic, obscure or ostentatious in writing. Scott once remarked '...there is very little written for a newspaper that would not be improved by being made shorter.' He always questioned 'Americanisms' such as 'final showdown', and would frequently change incorrect grammar in articles. However, he was always courteous to his staff and avoided making discouraging remarks.

CP rarely praised his staff because he expected them to get their satisfaction through their work. Scott had a number of favourite sayings about the staff such as 'he'll have to go' or 'most irregular'. Scott not only edited the paper but was also the owner after purchasing it in 1905.

His daily routine was to deal with correspondence during the day at home, with a break for an hour of cycling in the afternoon. Then in the evening at 6pm he arrived at the newspaper office. Until his late seventies he cycled in from his home 'The Firs' in Fallowfield. Later he drove into Manchester by car. He always brought with him two eggs, salt wrapped in paper, milk, and sometimes an apple. He then read through the evening papers in readiness for preparation of 'The Long' - the newspaper's leader article. This was for him the most important part of the paper which helped to influence public opinion. CP was generally left undisturbed while he was writing this.

On Scott's retirement in 1929 there were messages from the King, the Prime Minister, and the Archbishop of York in praise of his fifty-seven years at the Guardian. Lord Cecil said Scott '...had made righteousness readable'. The following year he received the Freedom of Manchester at the Town Hall. He died in 1932 aged 85, and his son, Edward, took over the editorship but died three years later in a boating accident on Lake Windermere, a few months after his father's death.

Scott receiving the Freedom of Manchester.

Right: As the last northern edition of the Manchester Guardian was being printed here at Cross Street in 1970, the editorial library containing 16,000 books and cuttings was removed, along with a previously locked cupboard which was said to have contained CP Scott's bicycle puncture kit.

Stephen Harrison worked as a temporary messenger here with the Manchester Evening News when Brian Redhead was the Editor. He recalls the pneumatic tube system which shot items around the open-plan office, and the thundering print presses deep in the basement. His weekly pay in 1970 was £4 11s 1d.

Below: Section of a street scene showing the Thatched House in 1823. It was by Joseph Parry (1744-1826) who was born in Liverpool but moved to Manchester in 1790 where he became known as the 'Father of Art'. The licensee at the inn was Robert Sykes.

Willow Publishing

Bonhams

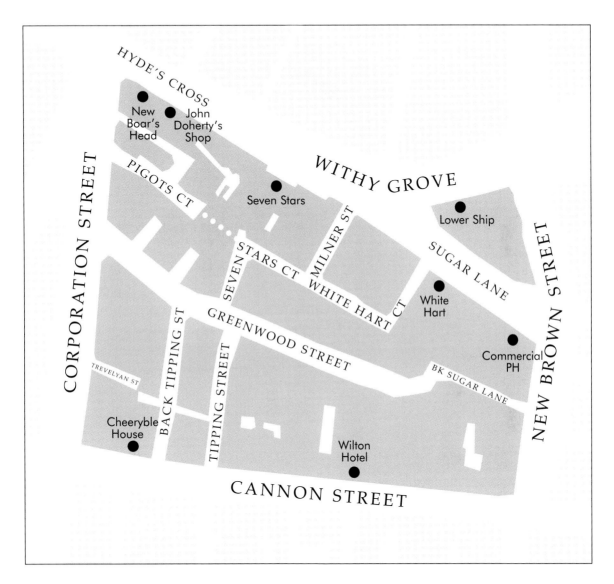

SECTION 4

THE WILTON HOTEL

The business at 35 Cannon Street became known as the Wilton Hotel in 1881, but around 1859, it was the Adelphi Beer and Chop-House. Emma Charlesworth purchased it in 1867 and three years later renamed it Charlesworth's Day Hotel and Restaurant. Surrounded by warehouses and other commercial buildings, the hotel was frequented by spinners and others coming into the city on market days. The 1871 Census indicates that fourteen women were employed at the hotel. Emma continued to run the hotel after her husband Robert died in 1873.

By 1879 John Nowell was the tenant, and in 1881 the business had gone into receivership. There had been issues with the safety of the hundred-year old building and business had decreased because of it. Parts of the structure were supported by props until repairs were eventually carried out. The hotel's fittings and furniture were auctioned in 1883, and then, the following year, the hotel and adjoining warehouse were pulled down and rebuilt. The new building re-opened in 1886 with a large restaurant and billiard room.

There was an explosion in the dining room in 1887. It had been caused by a young plumber who went to examine a gas leak and foolishly switched on a gas light before the room had been properly ventilated. As a result of the blast, part of the floor was torn up, and a waiter was knocked off his feet. The man was uninjured but downstairs, plaster came down, a table was broken and rooms were filled with clouds of dust.

The well-known professional billiards player John Roberts Junior played an exhibition match at the hotel in 1889. Roberts, born in Ardwick, gave

Manchester Libraries, Information and Archives

his opponent a 350 start before winning. He was one of the main players of his era and also manufactured billiard cues and tables. Roberts was a promoter of the sport and also involved in the setting of new rules.

The hotel's owner in 1903, Ralph Schultz, was from Scotland where he had been a wine and spirit merchant and licensee. He died in mysterious circumstances at the hotel. He was a heavy drinker and a man was employed to look after him. Schultz, age 52, was found slumped at the foot of the stairs and died a week later. At the inquest into his death, it was revealed there were unexplained bruises on his body. The jury returned an open verdict.

In 1930, nine men and a woman were arrested at the hotel on betting charges. At the Police Court hearing, a barman was fined £10 for allowing betting to take place, and a bookmaker was fined £25. It was announced in 1938 that the hotel was to be demolished as part of the Cannon Street road-widening scheme.

Greater Manchester Mueum of Transport Archives

CHEERYBLE HOUSE

Number 15 Cannon Street once belonged to the Grant Brothers who were immortalised in Charles Dickens' novel 'Nicholas Nickleby'. It had previously been the town house of the Peel family. The kind-hearted Cheeryble brothers in Dickens' story were said to have been inspired by William and Daniel Grant, the philanthropic merchants who carried on business here. The Grant family came from Scotland to Lancashire in 1783 and set up as calico printers in Manchester in 1800. There were four brothers in the business; William, the eldest and head of the firm was 'brother Ned' in the novel, Daniel 'brother Charles' who travelled around the north of England and Scotland obtaining orders, and Charles and John. The Grants bought Ramsbottom Print Works from Sir Robert Peel and began production in 1807. The business prospered both locally and in America and India. They were arguably one the best-known firms of Manchester calico printers. They were listed at Lower Cannon Street in 1812 and were at 15 Cannon Street by 1850. The firm continued there until about 1864.

There are many stories of the brothers' generosity. Perhaps the most moving are those where they have given to people who had wronged them in the past. The needy would wait outside the warehouse on Cannon Street for Daniel Grant to arrive in the morning, when either he or his clerk would distribute money to them. Their warehouse was visited by the Archdukes of Austria in 1815 during their tour of England and Scotland.

There has been much discussion as to whether Charles Dickens actually met the brothers. Dickens came to Manchester on a number of occasions but he states in the preface to the 1848 edition of 'Nicholas Nickelby' that he had 'never interchanged any communication in my life' with the Grants. This would seem to to be the end of the matter, except the precise Dickens' wording could mean he did not correspond with the brothers. He may have expressed it in that way to avoid further begging letters of which he had received many after the book's first edition. Thousands of letters and requests for loans were sent to him to be passed on to the Grants, after he had revealed they were real people. So many letters, as Dickens commented, it would have broken the Bank of England. However there was firm evidence that Dickens

and the Grants had all been at a dinner given by Gilbert Winter of The Stocks, Cheetham in January 1838. Also, William Keeling, a former President of the Manchester Academy, recalled being at the dinner and seeing Dickens and the Grants in conversation. There seems to have been another occasion when they met because it is recorded the brothers told their niece how they had been out to lunch with Dickens and had invited him to an evening meal but he had declined because of a prior engagement. Correspondence indicates that Dickens came to Manchester

Above: Cheeryble House before demolition.

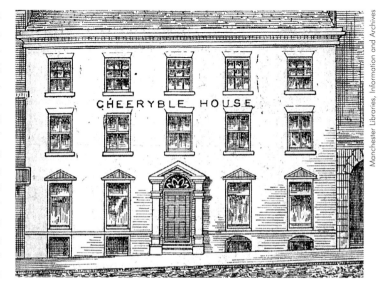

The Grants' former counting room.

the brothers as an inspiration and went on to develop the characters in the book in his own way. Others close to the Grants noticed individual traits of the brothers in the Cheerybles which suggested Dickens had observed them at close quarters. Although Dickens could have based his characters on what he had heard about the Grants, the evidence suggests it was written from first-hand experience.

By 1870 the basement of 15 Cannon Street was a restaurant, with the proprietress, Winefred Monahan, offering 'The best fourpenny beer in the City'. In 1900 the Manchester Improvement Committee announced that they were buying the historic warehouse in order to demolish it to widen Cannon Street. It was to be annually let until it was required for the road improvement.

The warehouse became known as Cheeryble House at the opening of Isaac Grundy's wallpaper and linoleum shop in 1900. Many of the building's interior features were retained, including a carved doorway, a chair and a safe from the days of the Grants. American visitors, and others interested in its links with Dickens, paid a visit to the old premises shortly before it was demolished in 1907. Grundy relocated to Blackfriars Street and the premises were used temporarily by a bank.

several times visiting mills to research a book but also to see his sister who lived in the city, as well as attending meetings in connection with Manchester's Free Libraries and the Athenaeum. People who knew the Grants said that Dickens' portrayal of them in his book was something of a caricature. Presumably the great novelist used

ISAAC NEWTON GRUNDY,

Merchant and Manufacturer of

PAPER HANGINGS

AND

DECORATIVE SPECIALITIES

For all Markets, Home, Colonial, and Foreign,

Sole Agent for the
"EMDECA" FLEXIBLE METALLIC TILES.

New Show Rooms now open for

CARPETS, LINOLEUMS, RUGS, ETC.

For both Wholesale and Retail Trades.

NOTE NEW ADDRESS—

CHEERYBLE HOUSE, 15, CANNON STREET

(One Minute from Old Address),

MANCHESTER.

CHEERYBLE HOUSE.
[Once the home of Dickens's immortal "Cheeryble Brothers."]

ESTABLISHED 1850.   Telegrams—"Hangings," Manchester.   Nat. Tel. 3120.

Above left: The old 'counting house' with safe in Cheeryble House from the days when it housed the Grants' warehouse.

Left: The owner, Mr Grundy, said that an old gentleman still visited the shop who had been formerly employed as a clerk by the Grant brothers. He dressed in 'John Bull' style with top boots and long waistcoat and used to stand on the top steps and distribute money to the poor.

HYDE'S CROSS

The 1650 map of Manchester shows the cross at the junction of Withy Grove, Hanging Ditch, Fennel Street and Toad Lane. Although it is depicted as a cross, it may have had a pinnacle similar to those at Market Place and in Salford.

The cross is thought to have been erected by the Hyde family in the 16th century. Hamo Hyde had lands in Manchester in 1525. Thomas Hyde was ordered in 1553 to remove a dung hill from his land on Toad Lane (Todd Street) which is the end of the lane where the cross was situated. Then in 1628 there is reference to 'lands in Hanging Ditch near to Hide Cross'. From then onwards the cross is frequently mentioned because it was a landmark. The date of 1653 on the shaft must have been when it was re-erected. The Court Leet Records in 1651 show there was an earlier gibbet in the market which was to be destroyed and replaced by Hyde's Cross in 1653. The gibbet or pillory had been erected during the Civil War.

The shaft is made of grey sandstone with the inscription MBWH·1653. 'MB' is thought to be Michael Buxton who was a member of the jury who ordered the gibbet to be destroyed. 'WH' is likely to be William Heawood who was steward of the Court Leet around the time of the gibbet's removal and the erection of the new cross. It had been removed by the 1770s because in 1775 the place was known as 'Hides Cross' without the definite article. Hyde's Cross became the name of the thoroughfare from Fennel Street up to Withy Grove, ending at Cock Gates.

The cross was acquired by John Hillkirk who was surveyor and agent to the Lord of the Manor, Sir Oswald Mosley. Hillkirk preserved this highly-prized relic in his garden at Beswick Lodge, then after his death his son, John Jnr, removed it to his garden in Withington where it remained until 1896. It then passed into the ownership of his son-in-law Professor Robert Wild in Fallowfield who presented it to Chetham's in 1913. During the building of Corporation Street, the base of an old cross was excavated, which was possibly for the shaft now at Chetham's.

Hyde's Cross at Chetham's.

The first mention of a market at Hyde's Cross occurs in Court Leet records in 1665 when it was ordered that pigs could only be sold there and nowhere else. Inhabitants at Hyde's Cross were complaining about the nuisance of the market in 1748. In response, the potato market was removed to the upper part of 'Withen Grove'. This was also the first time the modern wording of Hyde's Cross was used, previously it had been 'Hide' or 'Hyde'. A pig sty erected there in 1755 was ordered to be removed, suggesting the swine had also become an annoyance.

Helen Webster

The corner of Hyde's Cross and Corporation Street. Note the old Hyde's Cross street sign on the wall.

Sanctuary Cross

Because of its proximity to the Collegiate Church some have thought that Hyde's Cross may have been a sanctuary cross. Until the Reformation, fugitives from justice believed they wouldn't be arrested if they were within a mile radius of a church. The cross marked the boundary of the 'safe area'. After the dissolution of the monasteries in 1540, following an Act of Parliament, Manchester became one of eight towns designated as a place of asylum or sanctuary. Several sanctuary houses with altars were set up in Manchester which each sheltered up to twenty people. There was said to be one at Hyde's Cross opposite the Old Boar's Head.

The people of Manchester did not appreciate having so many criminals in their midst and the 'privilege' of being a sanctuary town was transferred to Chester.

The hotel in 1920.

NEW BOAR'S HEAD

The inn at Hyde's Cross was licensed in 1793, and situated opposite the Old Boar's Head which was licensed earlier in 1654. A crowd gathered at the New Boar's Head in October 1833 for the sale of a wooden table. The table belonged to John Doherty whose shop was a few doors away (See John Doherty) but it had been seized by Mr Horner, the tax collector, in lieu of non-payment of £1.2s.6d. house and window duties. This unpopular tax was opposed by many and Doherty organised three hundred supporters to go to the tavern to prevent the sale of his table taking place.

Their disruption caused the sale of the table to be delayed and go beyond the permitted five days for it to be sold. The table then became the property of its original owner, and it was carried shoulder-high back to Doherty's shop where it was presented to his wife as 'the gift of the people'. However Doherty wisely decided to reject it as it may have been regarded as felony and the table was returned to the New Boar's Head. The table disappeared from the pub overnight and was found the following morning standing outside. The tax collector hoped he would be able to go ahead with the sale but the table leaves had been removed during the protests and the landlord found himself liable for the damage to the table.

A man described as 'respectable looking' walked into the New Boar's Head in October 1901 and began firing a gun. Customers fled and the police were called. PC W Hewitt arrived and bravely arrested the man, whose name was James Boardman. The gunman, a pork butcher from Radcliffe, had been drinking heavily and was firing blank cartridges. He said he had bought the gun to scare his wife, from whom he was separated, and had to pay £2 a week. A doctor who knew him later testified that Boardman was easily affected by alcohol. He was bound over to keep the peace and fined £10. Before the pub was demolished, the Bull's Head carving on the frontage was removed and reported to have been given to a museum in Leeds in 1975. However its whereabouts are not known today.

The Peterloo Spy on Withy Grove

Prior to the infamous Peterloo incident, the organisers held a number of meetings in order to work out strategies to keep the crowds in an orderly fashion. They were aware their opponents would try to brand the meeting as unruly and out of control, and so they asked that everyone who was to attend the big meeting should be sober.

James Murray, a gingerbread maker at 2 Withy Grove, was not only a special constable but also a government spy. Disguised as a weaver, he watched the training sessions which were supervised by an old soldier. Murray was recognised by some of the organisers and the cry went up 'Spy!'. He was beaten up before staggering back to his home.

The incident further convinced local magistrates of the likelihood of violence at the forthcoming meeting at St Peter's Field and they issued a notice forbidding women and children to attend.

On the day of Peterloo, Henry Hunt, who was to speak at the meeting, and the crowd following him along Shudehill, stopped outside Murray's house to voice their disapproval of his spying activities. Later, as word spread of Murray's actions, people boycotted his shop and he was forced to retire.

Henry Hunt

Willow Publishing

The Seven Stars Inn, one of Manchester's oldest inns, controversially pulled down in 1911.

Willow Publishing

Outside the Lower Ship Inn, Withy Grove. The Pattreiouex company, opposite, later issued cards with their cigarettes.

Withy Grove

'The Withingreave' was once a pleasant country lane surrounded by fields. 'Withen' is a local name for 'withy', a species of willow. 'Greave' means 'hollow in the ground' where willows grew. There was a stream to one side which ran into the Irwell. Withens or withies were used in the construction of half-timbered buildings.

The withies were woven into the framework and then covered in clay or daub.

In 1569 Roger Bexwicke was a farmer at Withingreave, paying eight shillings a year rent to the Lord of the Manor. The Court Leet records in the early 1670s indicate Humphrey Chetham and Thomas Berron were instructed to remove a dung heap and rubbish off the lane opposite their properties.

John Doherty - fiery campaigner

Doherty (1798-1854), one of Manchester's great radical campaigners, had a bookshop and printers at 4 Withy Grove in the 1830s. He came from Ireland in 1816 as a cotton spinner to obtain better wages and soon became involved in trade union activities. For most of his life, he campaigned for factory reform and worker's rights.

He was self-taught, but he was an eloquent and passionate speaker, and a good organiser and he led several strikes including the protest at Murray's New Mill in 1818. He was imprisoned at Lancaster in 1818 for his involvement in preventing 'scabs' or 'knobsticks' returning to work at Birley's Mill. Despite being sentenced to two years' hard labour, he continued to campaign and write. Following a libel dispute with a Stockport clergyman whom he accused of 'body snatching' he was sent to prison for two months.

He led Manchester spinners in a six-month strike against wage cuts in 1829, and tried to establish a national union of spinners, and a union of all trades. Doherty was a frequent speaker in support of the Ten Hours Bill and gave evidence to a Parliamentary Select Committee on trade unionism.

His first office was on the opposite side of Shudehill, printing and selling religious and radical books. Then in 1834 he moved to bigger premises next to the New Boar's Head (See New Boar's Head - Doherty's table). It was known as Doherty's London Periodical Office where, for the price of a penny, customers had access to over ninety newspapers and magazines of the day. They could also pay extra for coffee, tea and light refreshments. Amongst the publications was the 'Mirror of Parliament' which recorded Westminster debates. This was a competitor to Hansard, with Charles Dickens as one of its reporters, a nephew of the owner of the publication.

Doherty was involved in publishing a number of newspapers which strongly argued the case for better workers' conditions. None of them lasted long but the titles such as 'The Voice of the People' and

Manchester cotton operatives.

'The Workman's Expositor' reflected the content. Perhaps the most famous of them was the 'Poor Man's Advocate'. He pressed for temperance and Irish self-rule and was much involved in Manchester politics.

He was fiery and fearless, and his home life was equally turbulent. His wife Laura stabbed him in the arm following her frustration over his neglect of domestic duties. After his death in 1854, his devotion to the welfare of others was recognised by Lord Salisbury who wrote 'No-one could have been more faithful to the cause.'

Bystanders gather for the photographer outside the Seven Stars c1903.

THE SEVEN STARS

Both the claims about the building's history and its contents are questionable. The sign outside proclaimed it to be the oldest licensed house in Great Britain having been licensed for over 540 years. Records reportedly seen at the County Record Office in 1867 stated that the first licence was granted in 1356 during the reign of Edward III. However, licences were only introduced for ale houses and 'tippling houses' in 1552. Before then, ale could be served in any location without permission. Nevertheless the Seven Stars had been licensed for an impressive three and a half centuries and could have been an unlicensed hostelry in the years before.

Robert Crook, proprietor of the inn for sixteen years, published a booklet about the stories and traditions of the old inn. Several pages are given to Guy Fawkes's visit to the Seven Stars. Fawkes was supposed to have hidden here, and there was a room named after him. This idea came from a novel by Harrison Ainsworth and is not historically accurate.

There were claims that an arch in the cellars was once an entrance to an underground passage to the Cathedral, but there was no evidence for this. Old silver plates found in a cupboard in the bar in 1885 during structural alterations were said to have been left there by dragoons during the Civil War but on expert examination were found to be of a much later date and made in Sheffield. The Seven Stars does have some historical associations. The 1745 Court Leet Records mention 5s 6d payment for horses by John Hulme during the time of the visit of Charles Stuart, when soldiers under the command of Colonel Townley are said to have slept there.

Top left and right: The Vestry was once the meeting place of the gentlemen of the 'Watch and Ward'. The chief of this group used to say 'Now we will go on our rounds, and then have another glass'. The Vestry had a cupboard which had not been opened for many years. The room also contained a 'man trap', leg irons, and folding prison doors presented to the proprietor of the Seven Stars by the Lancashire & Yorkshire Railway in 1872, after they had taken over the New Bailey Prison site. (See page 142)

Middle: The Dining Room contained the Cromwell chair and table where Roundhead soldiers sat while said to be quartered here.

Below: The Bar Parlour had an oak settle dated 1728 and a 17th century chair.

Sign origin

The sign of the 'Seven Stars' probably had masonic associations, with the circle of six stars and star in the middle. This was derived from the Bible where in the book of Revelation in chapter one, verse sixteen it refers to a Messianic figure holding seven stars.

The Seven Stars c1910. To the right is Thomas Tallis Ltd, cheese factors. Thomas was born at Hawarden and established his business in 1892. He was an expert on Cheshire cheese and lived in Cheadle Hulme. He retired to Wem in Shropshire where he died in 1926.

Benjamin Tayler was the inn-keeper at the time of Manchester's first directory in 1772. James Hudson was the landlord for thirty two years, and died in 1854. The licence passed to Sarah Hudson who continued there until her death in 1865.

In 1899 rumours began to circulate that the inn was to be demolished and rebuilt, but the two owners who lived in the south of England gave reassurances that they had no plans to change it. But in 1911 many were shocked to learn the lease of the Seven Stars had expired and that the inn was to be demolished to make way for warehouses. The Secretary of the National Trust wrote to the Manchester Guardian expressing concern that there seemed to have been little effort to save it and suggested it should be preserved. The Manchester Parks Committee refused to rebuild the frontage in any of its parks. A newspaper writer commented 'It is one of the few buildings we have left which enable us to visualise the Manchester of our great-grandfathers.' Another correspondent wrote 'To tear it down would be to deprive not only ourselves but future generations of something which a wilderness of warehouses could not compensate.'

Crucially, the Council did not act to save it and demolition went ahead. As it was being knocked down in June 1911 the Manchester City News reported 'Early in the week unsympathetic workmen, dust-begrimed, were tearing out the inner fittings, and despite the busy hammering, there was an air of melancholy about the place... The inner existence of 'Ye Olde Seven Stars' was departing with a crash, and soon its outer shell will be added to the things that have been.' During demolition a quantity of old coins was found beneath the floor in an upper room, including a copper coin reputedly 400 years old.

By 1900 there was great concern in Manchester that many
of its historic sites were under threat including the Seven Stars,
as shown in this Manchester Evening Chronicle cartoon.

Willow Publishing

The Sitting Room of the Seven Stars had a chair said to have belonged to John Bunyan who became a non-conformist preacher. For this he was imprisoned and during his time there wrote 'Pilgrim's Progress'.

Auction of the Seven Stars' treasures

When landlord Robert Crook retired in 1907, there were some interesting pieces of furniture and other curiosities from the inn amongst the 250 items being auctioned:

● A chair with the inscription 'Richard Lumley, Viscount Lumley of Waterford' dated 1615 with the family coat of arms. The top of the chair read 'Drede God' and lower down 'God spare our noble Kynge'. There was a carving on the back of the King of Scotland taking the oath of allegiance to Edward I, and the family motto 'a sound conscience is a wall of brass'.

● An armchair from Newstead Abbey in Nottinghamshire, the home of the poet Lord Byron, and a long case clock which had stood at the top of the stairs of the inn for 300 years and was still working.

● An iron alms box from Manchester Cathedral with double locks which needed two people to open it.

● Prison doors from the New Bailey Prison, Salford where three men known as the Manchester Martyrs, during the campaign for Irish Home Rule, were imprisoned and executed in 1867 after their armed attack in Hyde Road to rescue their compatriots from a police van, and for the killing a policeman.

● A man-trap, an instrument of torture belonging to the ancestors of Sir Humphrey de Trafford.

SUGAR LANE

The Collegiate Church registers first mention the lane in 1605 when Richard Boile, a plague victim of Sugar Lane, was buried. It was referred to in the Court Leet records of 1738 when John Holme was fined for not removing an obstruction. The lane is shown on Casson and Berry's 1746 map but not named.

An ancient water pipe was discovered at the corner of Sugar Lane and New Brown Street in 1905. During excavations, workmen found three lengths of hollowed-out tree trunks. Joints had been formed by thinning one end of the trunk to fit into the next one. The conduit could have been 200 years old and was thought to have conveyed water from one of the springs in Spring Gardens to homes in Shudehill.

Ancient water pipe uncovered.

WHITE HART

Around 1772 cattle sales were held on Saturdays outside the pub at 16 Sugar Lane. When auctioned in 1827 the property included a shop, rooms over the court or gateway, detached kitchen, yard, brewhouse and two stables. The inn had been demolished by 1867 but the name of White Hart Court was retained.

WEAVERS' ARMS

From about 1779 to 1829 the inn at 10 Sugar Lane had been known as the Weavers' Arms. In 1787, it was the venue for a public debate with the question discussed: 'Whether do real or imaginary evils more agitate the mind'.

In 1796 the inn was a recruiting station for Sergeant Aylward of the 'Noble, Free, and Spirited Manchester Corps of Marines'. France had declared war on England the previous year and men were needed both onshore and afloat. Marines were trained as soldiers but paid by the Admiralty. Manchester raised its own company of over a thousand marines, including some from Liverpool and North Wales who went to serve on various fighting ships.

A broadsheet appealed for recruits, offering ten guineas to those whose 'hearts beat for the glory and fortune at the sound of the warlike drum.' Recruits were offered comfortable barracks, with as much meat and drink as they wished, and when on board ship, they would have strong grog, and the prospect of making their fortunes. They would enter into immediate pay and 'meet with high dashing fellows who are able to manage a musket or cannon, scorn fear, laugh at fear, and set death at defiance.' The company were also wanting 'a number of fine handsome young fellows for sergeants and corporals.'

Their commanding officer was John Lees of Oldham, who, when he officially received the company colours at a church ceremony, was reported to have said, 'We receiven these flags wi' gratitude. We'n defend 'em wi' fortitude, an' if th' French shooten th' rags away we'n bring the poles back!' In the 1820s the licensee was Mrs Cowdroy, wife of William, a printer and publisher who founded the Gazette which was later bought by Archibald Prentice. (See Manchester Examiner Offices)

NAME CHANGES

The publican of the Weavers' Arms was accused of keeping a disorderly house in 1829, and some time between 1832 and 1836 it changed its name to the Commercial Inn. It was re-named again in 1944 to the Sugar Loaf because the licensee had grown tired of people, including American servicemen, knocking on the door for accommodation at all hours. In those times, 'Commercial' indicated a place where you could get a bed for the night. Inside, there was a low beamed ceiling and an ancient grandfather clock. An old ship's brass bell hung from the ceiling. Mrs May Kelland was the licensee in 1962. It had extended opening hours for newspaper workers. Two other pubs known of in Sugar Lane were the Crown and Cushion 1772, and the Black Dog which existed in the 1850s and 60s.

The Sugar Loaf 1970.

The corner of Sugar Lane and New Brown Street, looking towards Withy Grove.

144

Manchester Libraries, Information and Archives

Greenwood Street in 1938 near the junction of Seven Stars Court on the left. Greenwood Street was named after John Greenwood, a bed quilt, counterpane and muslin manufacturer who built four warehouses here about 1828. His business premises were at 6 Cromford Court in 1821.

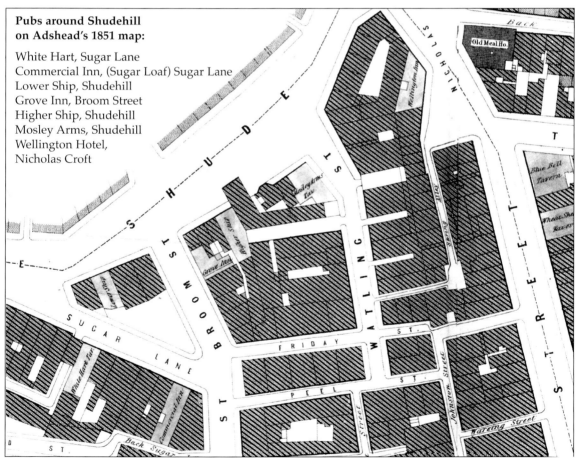

Pubs around Shudehill on Adshead's 1851 map:

White Hart, Sugar Lane
Commercial Inn, (Sugar Loaf) Sugar Lane
Lower Ship, Shudehill
Grove Inn, Broom Street
Higher Ship, Shudehill
Mosley Arms, Shudehill
Wellington Hotel,
Nicholas Croft

LOWER SHIP INN

The Lower Ship Inn, prior to demolition 1970.

The deeds go back to 1777 and it was possibly an ale house in 1721. Its earliest address was 22 Sugar Lane but after later re-numbering, it was at 6a Sugar Lane accessed through a passage with an entrance at 34 Withy Grove. By 1800 it was known as 'The Old Ship'.

In the 1861 Census, there were 11 people lodging there. Abel Heywood held a meeting there in July 1865 and was unanimously nominated as an MP for Manchester. When the business was sold in 1874, the advertisement mentioned the 'splendid concert room'. Several inns in the locality had concert rooms where there were nightly entertainments.

They were entertained by professional singers as well as the regulars. The customers preferred songs with good choruses which they could join in, and sentimental ballads, after a few drinks. By 1877 the Lower Ship became known as the Lloyds Hotel, then reverted to its previous name about 1882.

Musical entertainment in the pub concert room. Drawing by Jack Yates 1906.

In 1907 objections were made to the renewal of its licence because of the disorderly behaviour of certain women customers. The licensee, John Hague, said that he was a total abstainer and that the house previously held a clear record for twenty years. The licence was renewed on condition the two back doors were closed, with no drinking in the passage and that it could only open six days a week, closing at 10pm. The pub was not granted a full licence until 1952. The landlord's living quarters looked down onto the bar, and there was a claim that Dick Turpin hid here.

Abel Heywood - Manchester Man

Abel Heywood (1810-1893) was one of Manchester's best-loved citizens who had a long association with the city. He was born in Prestwich, then came to Manchester where he set up a penny reading room in Oldham Street in 1831. The following year he became an agent for the 'Poor Man's Guardian' which represented the views of the National Association of Working Classes.

In order to suppress public opinion, a levy was imposed on newspapers but Heywood refused to have his paper taxed and was fined £54. Instead of the tax stamp in the corner of the publication, the newspaper had the words 'Knowledge is power'. After refusing to pay the fine he was sentenced to four months in the New Bailey Prison, Salford in 1832.

In his letters from prison he complained about the hard beds and the food 'that was not fit for pigs'. The newspaper continued to be sold while he was in prison and then after his release. For this he was fined twice more and paid fines totalling £18. It was claimed that 750 people were jailed for selling untaxed copies of the Poor Man's Guardian. Thanks to the agitation of Heywood and others, the four pence tax was reduced to one penny in 1836 and completely abolished in 1855.

Heywood stood for Parliament in 1859 and 1865 as a Radical Liberal candidate but was not successful. He was closely involved in the civic life of the city and was on the paving and sanitation committee of the Police Commissioners for many years. Heywood actively campaigned for the incorporation of the borough and was elected to the council in 1843. For almost fifty years he was chairman of the Highways Committee.

He was closely involved in the building of the new Town Hall which he officially opened during his second term as Mayor. There was a lavish reception and a great trades procession by workers in tribute to Heywood. The bell in the clock tower was named after him. 'Great Abel', which first rang in 1879 is inscribed with his initials and with the words of Tennyson 'Ring out the false, ring in the true'.

During 1842 there was rioting in Manchester, and cannons were placed on the main streets, along with armed military. Five of the rioters came into Heywood's shop and took some goods. With the help of another man he gave chase and managed to capture one of them as they divided the spoils. For his actions he was commended by the government for promoting law and order.

Heywood was also a noted bookseller and publisher in the city. Among his newspapers was the weekly 'Manchester Spectator' first published in 1849. He became nationally known for his 'Penny Guides' as people began to travel around by train. He joined a company manufacturing wallpaper which sold the product in its millions.

Towards the end of his life he was honoured for his public service with a banquet at the Town Hall in 1888. He was granted the freedom of the city in 1891 after looking after its streets for so many years. On his eightieth birthday he was presented with a silver gilt casket at the Manchester Reform Club, of which he was president, for his years of campaigning for liberty and justice. He was known as 'The Father of Manchester Corporation' and it was said of him that 'no man ever died more unanimously honoured in his own locality.'

NEW BROWN STREET

Previously known as Broom(e) Street in 1764 when Mr Desaubrys was advertising tickets for his ball, on sale at Mrs Walker's house.

The New Manchester Subscription Library began at 10 Broome Street in 1792 under the name of 'The Manchester Reading Society', then two years later 'The New Manchester Library' before coming to be known as the 'Royal Exchange Library'. It initially opened three evenings a week to subscribers. Critics denounced it as 'The Jacobin Library' because of the views of some of its promoters. There were even suggestions it would be raided in search of controversial publications. The founders of the library were forced to confirm there were no seditious volumes within the collection.

Withy Grove stores on the corner of New Brown Street and Withy Grove, 1958.

By 1797 the library contained 328 books, including 18 volumes of Encyclopedia Britannica. The Library, after moving from Broome Street, was located at Pool Fold and St Ann's Street before coming to Manchester Royal Exchange. Then in 1854 it transferred to Cross Street and next to 57 King Street before its final move to 50 King Street West in 1893. It closed five years later and sold off its 40,000 books.

Manchester Libraries

The Old Manchester Subscription Library was open during this period. This was established c1765 and closed in 1867. In 1844 the combined stocks of the two subscription libraries along with Chetham's Library totalled 66,000 volumes. Chetham's Library had been established in 1655, and its collection has been designated of national and international importance.

The Portico independent subscription library on Mosley Street was established in 1806 by a group of Manchester businessmen. In the 1820s the Law Library and the Mechanics' Institute Library also opened. As Manchester became a more cosmopolitan city, the British and Foreign Library was founded in 1830 at Bridge Street with works in Italian, French and German. In 1903 it handed over its collection of 14,000 books to Manchester Corporation for the nominal amount of £65.

Following the 1850 Public Libraries Act Manchester established the free reference and lending libraries which opened in 1852. Charles Dickens, radical politician John Bright and the novelist William Thackeray attended the official opening at Campfield.

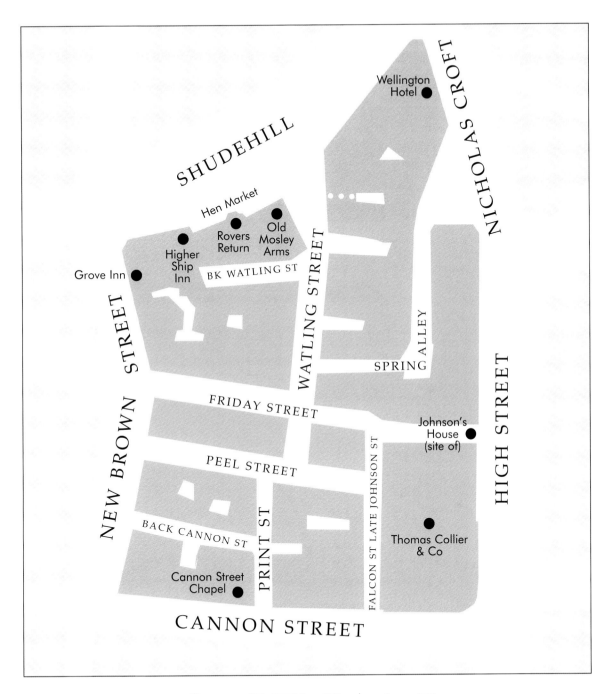

SECTION 5

Willow Publishing

The chapel building after it had been converted into business premises.

CANNON STREET CHAPEL

This was the only place of Christian worship within the 'Lost District' although there were other non-conformist chapels nearby. Several churches around the city were formed from the congregations here. The chapel, at what was then known as Hunter's Croft, was completed in 1761 and licensed for worship in 1762. The building and the gallery cost £492 18s 11d to construct. It was set amongst former gardens and orchards belonging to householders in High Street and

Marsden Square. Caleb Warhurst, the first minister, previously assisted James Winterbottom at Coldhouse (originally 'Cold Arse') Chapel at Thorniley Brow. Warhurst, the son of a carpenter in Bredbury, Stockport, was ordained in 1756. He won many new converts who became part of his new congregation at Cannon Street. His friend, John Newton, who was associated with many of the leading Dissenters of the time and who wrote the hymn 'Amazing Grace', attended the chapel opening. Warhurst died of consumption in 1765 at the age of forty-three, and was buried beneath the pulpit of the chapel. There were 110 people attending the church at that time. His successor, Rev Timothy Priestley, was also an outstanding preacher and remained there for eighteen years. He was a controversial character, and frequently chastised by the church elders for his behaviour. On one occasion he was late coming to a service and conducted worship still wearing a hat. In protest against his small stipend, he earned extra income by making packing cases and selling alcohol. The chapel was enlarged during the time of his ministry, with the demolition of two cottages in front of the chapel.

Rev David Bradbury

Priestley was dismissed in 1784 and went on to became pastor of an Independent Church in London. He also published and edited several Christian journals as well as producing an annotated family bible. Priestley's elder brother, Joseph, was a Unitarian and they frequently argued over their theological differences. However they worked together on various electrical devices including a kite and a machine which produced electrostatic charges. David Bradbury (or Bradberry) was appointed minister in 1785. He supplemented his income by writing epic poems. His stay was marred by disputes among rival factions within the church, and his battles with the church elders who tried to remove him from office. In 1788 many of the church members at Cannon Street left to meet at a newly-built chapel on Mosley Street. Then in 1848 they moved again to the Cavendish Street chapel which was nicknamed 'the carriage road to heaven' because of the wealthy families who attended it. By about 1795 Bradbury had moved to a chapel in London.

William Roby, the next minister at Cannon Street around 1795, was much more popular and, as the congregation increased, Roby left in 1807 with

Rev Timothy Priestley

Rev William Roby

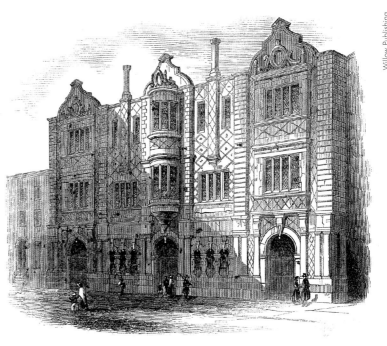

Roby's Day and Sunday Schools off Piccadilly.

151

many of them and went to the newly-built Grosvenor Street Chapel, off Piccadilly where he helped to establish many new churches across the North West, and train new ministers.

Attendances at the Cannon Street Chapel grew once again and it was rebuilt in 1828. Afterwards there was great change as church members gradually moved out of the centre of Manchester. Homes were lost in the Cannon Street area as more commercial premises were built. The chapel was sold for £2800 in 1860. The congregation used temporary accommodation before moving to a new church at Chorlton Road, Old Trafford.

The chapel building on Cannon Street was sold in 1860 and two years later used as a yarn warehouse. The pulpit and pews were sold, and the floor flagged over. The chapel-keeper's house on Print Street and a building on Back Cannon Street, used as a vestry and school, were also made into commercial premises. The rear yard of the

chapel contained graves and was covered over. and used as a wheelwright's yard. The Corporation's Health Committee ordered the owners to clean up the yard and remove rubbish. When the graves were revealed, it was found that all the inscriptions had been chiselled away. Members of the Chorlton Road Church met in the old Cannon Street building in 1938 to hold a service of thanksgiving for the founders of the church.

One of the rooms in the former chapel could only be entered though a trapdoor. In 1939 it was amongst a block of buildings demolished in order to widen Cannon Street. During demolition, a wall collapsed, killing two workmen, and injuring two others and a passing motorist as it showered the street in debris. The coffins from the old chapel were moved to Southern Cemetery after Manchester Corporation obtained a special Act of Parliament. The coffins seemed to have been piled five or six deep and crumbled as soon they were uncovered.

Kaiserman Collection

The north side of Cannon Street looking towards High Street, with the old chapel at the top.

PEEL STREET

The Peel family had built a number of warehouses there by 1788 in the new street. They had close associations with Manchester, beginning with Robert Peel (1723-1795), mill owner and grandfather of future prime minister Sir Robert Peel who helped to create the forerunner of today's police force. He was also instrumental in the repeal of the Corn Laws which kept bread prices high to protect the landowners' interests.

ROBERT PEEL THE ELDER

Robert Peel the elder was born in Oswaldtwistle at Peele Fold. His father was a farmer, although his grandfather had made woollen cloth. Robert, after leaving school, experimented with printing on wool with old wood blocks he had inherited from his grandfather. He became one of the earliest calico-printers in Lancashire and had a warehouse in Manchester and a mill in Blackburn about 1750.

Peel enjoyed trying out new techniques and introduced a sprig of parsley into the pattern on a printed plate. The design became popular and led to his nickname of 'Parsley Peel'. He worked with James Hargreaves, who later invented the Spinning Jenny, to develop new technology, but the new machinery was destroyed by rioters in 1779. He moved his business to Burton-on-Trent where he was again targeted by rioters. Afterwards, he introduced Richard Arkwright's carding engine which brought great success. In his later years, Peel lived at Ardwick to be with his daughter. He left his estate to his eight children, who became the equivalent of today's millionaires.

ROBERT PEEL, JNR

Robert Peel's third son, Robert (1750-1830), set up a calico printing business in 1770. The first mill was at Blackburn before Peel moved to Bury. He also had cotton mills at Tamworth where he was MP. He was made a Baronet in 1800. By 1782 his

The street's old oval stone name sign, measuring 32in by 25in, had been built into one of the houses in the thoroughfare. During the widening of Cannon Street a similar sign was given to Manchester Museum in 1939, but this cannot now be located.

company was also listed at Cannon Street, Manchester, with another warehouse in St Ann's Square and offices on Half Moon Street. Peel moved from his warehouse in St Ann's Square in 1788 to Peel Street, and also from his Cannon Street premises to Peel Street in 1794.

Over the following decades, various members of the Peel family had businesses here or in neighbouring Watling Street. Peel and Co had 23 mills in the North West by 1795. People remembered that the first warehouse off Cannon Street was approached by an avenue of trees. Deliveries from the mill were made three times a week with crowds of drapers coming into the showrooms to buy the new designs. They scrambled for the latest prints and put their purchases into piles to be costed by clerks.

GROVE INN

Manchester Libraries, Information and Archives

and Westmoreland Wrestling Society, who were holding the annual sports at the Circus, Peter Street. The best wrestlers in England competed and there was also a 'pole leaping contest'.

By the 1960s the inn was known as 'the newspaper pub', not only because it was frequented by newspaper workers but also for the large number of old newspapers displayed on the walls, including the first issue of an old Aberdeen paper. Also on show were press photos, cartoons and caricatures of historic and sporting significance. There was an upstairs meeting room used for newspaper union meetings. It had appropriately chapel-shaped windows for the meetings of the various 'chapels'. The licensee in 1963, Eileen Naughton, said that her upstairs dining room had once been a bar.

This was earlier known as the Fox in 1788, then later the Fox and Goose, at 2 Broome Street, afterwards becoming New Brown Street. It was known as the Grove Inn about 1837 when it was offering wines, spirits and accommodation. In 1854 it was used during the Municipal Elections as the office of William Turnbull, a flax spinner at Cannon Street, who was standing for the Exchange Ward.

The following year various items were on display at the inn, belonging to a Russian soldier killed during the Anglo-French bombardment of the fortress at Bomarsund. These included his musket, a bayonet and sword in black leather sheaths, and a sheepskin cloak. His helmet, decorated with two crossed cannons, was considered too small for most Englishmen to wear. The inn was then run by William Newton and continued in the family until 1871. In 1874 it was the committee rooms for the Cumberland

Street names

NICHOLAS CROFT
Named after Nicholas Mosley, who was Lord of the Manor of Manchester. The old Market Cross which originally stood opposite the Old Shambles was moved to Nicholas Croft after 1752 when the original cross was replaced by a more ornate version. It eventually fell to pieces and disappeared.

FRIDAY STREET
Part of the former Sugar Lane and shown on Laurent's 1793 map. The name was possibly derived from a London street of that name from the 1720s. Fish was sold there in London on the days when eating meat was forbidden.

WATLING STREET
It was in existence by 1793. At number three, in 1856, was the Nitro-Organic Manure Company, manufactured under the direction of Dr Edward Frankland (1825-1899), Professor of Chemistry at Owens College, Manchester. He was knighted in 1897 for his work on the purification of drinking water.

Part of the 1753 Hulme Charity document showing Withingreave Hall.

ROVER'S RETURN

Claims that it was the oldest beerhouse in Manchester dating from 1306 cannot be substantiated. It was not included in a 1905 list of the oldest licensed houses still in existence, which had opened between 1443 and 1799.

The old building which housed both the Rover's Return and Old Mosley Arms would seem to have been the former Withingreave Hall. The 1753 plan of the Hulme's Charity lands has a detailed drawing of the Hall property (See the section above). From this and later illustrations of the hall, we can conclude that the two public houses and adjoining premises were situated within the old Withingreave Hall.

After Hulme's death in 1691 the hall had a series of tenants who would not have used it as an inn. The rent role of 1710 indicated James Hilton was the tenant and he remained there until his death in 1763. The sale details of the property that year show there were also a number of cottages but there are no records of an alehouse there.

In 1795, the rates records indicate the left-hand side of the hall was occupied by the Old Mosley Arms and that the remaining section was listed as a house and warehouse. For the next twenty-four years various tenants including fruit-sellers were listed next door to the pub, then by 1829, the premises were opened as a public house and brew-house by Samuel Wilson. It was not known as the Rover's Return until about 1869 when the licensee, John Worrell, was offering a £50 reward to anyone who could prove he had allowed any wrongdoing in his public house. The pub's name probably originates from the words of the old folk song 'The Wild Rover' which tells of the return of the 'prodigal' laden with gold. Worrell also sold 'novelty' items and could have given the pub a name and a history to attract customers and to rival the nearby Seven Stars.

The Rover's Return was for sale in 1908 with a view to demolition and replacement by warehouses, but it was withdrawn from auction and the licence renewed in 1909.

It closed in 1923 after its licence, then held by Jessie Pearson, was referred to the Inland Revenue Commissioners. It remained untenanted until 1928 when the premises were opened as dining rooms by Edward Wharton. Florence Tredaway took over the café in 1936.

The Hulme Trust was wanting to sell the property when in 1939 fire destroyed the ground floor. Francis Shaw, a licensed broker, re-opened it as a shop selling second-hand goods about 1942. He was an ARP warden in Withy Grove and was commended for his bravery during the war .

In 1957 the building was declared unsafe by the owners, the Hulme Trust Estate, who applied to Manchester Corporation for a demolition order The last remaining section of the former Withingreave Hall was taken down in the spring of the following year. There were claims of underground passages from the brick-vaulted cellar to the river and the cathedral from the old pub. The pub's name lives on in TV's Coronation Street.

Withingreave Hall

Withingreave Hall was the town house of the Hulmes of Reddish. William Hulme founded an educational charity, the Hulme Trust in 1691, which included the Withingreave property, as well as other land in Manchester and outlying townships, to provide income to support Manchester students at Oxford University, and the livings of about 30 clergymen as well as establishing schools in Manchester, Oldham and Bury and scholarships at Owen's College.

The 1650 map of Manchester shows buildings at Withingreave surrounded by open fields. Surveys of the property in 1710 and 1753 by the Hulme Trustees indicated that merchant James Hilton was the tenant. It included out-buildings, an orchard and garden, cottages converted from a barn, stables and coach house, all set in 8 acres. It was for sale in 1763 after Hilton's death.

Willow Publishing

Shudehill with the Rovers Return just visible on the right hand side.

The Rover's Return, in the former medieval timber-framed house. The bay windows were added in late 18th century.

Poultry market on Shudehill outside the Mosley Arms and Rover's Return.

Willow Publishing

Manchester Libraries, Information and Archives

The Old Mosley Arms on the corner of Watling Street and Shudehill was substantially altered about 1860.

OLD MOSLEY ARMS

The Old Mosley Arms, in part of the former Withingreave Hall, was listed in the 1795 rates records with Thomas Amery the licensee. The Mosley Arms sale in 1804, confirmed that the pub was on a plot of land held by the Trustees of Hulme's Charity and was also suitable for conversion into warehouses or shops.

Isaac Gleave, the publican in 1829, was on the committee of the Manchester Philanthropic Society formed in 1811. This was an early form of trades union composed of trades people who set up a fund to help workers in financial distress. The Society closed in 1834.

The pub was named after the Mosley family who purchased the manor of Manchester from John Layce during the reign of Elizabeth I. For the sum of £3,500 Rowland and Nicholas Mosley acquired the markets, manors, lordships, fairs and tolls in 1596. Nicholas became Lord of the Manor

and was also Lord Mayor of London in 1599. He was knighted by Queen Elizabeth I and had a house at Hough End, Manchester. The Mosley family sold the manor to Manchester Corporation in 1845 for £200,000 paid by annual instalments. In its latter days the pub was popular with newspaper workers until its closure in the early 1970s.

Higher Ship Inn

The inn on Shudehill was licensed in 1763. It had been extended by 1877, and became Gradwell's Day Hotel and Restaurant. The owner, Samuel Gradwell died in 1900. He was a friend of Lancashire poet and writer Ben Brierley, and owner of housing property around Manchester. Gradwell bequeathed that the restaurant should be run by trustees and the profits given to his 34 employees, then after seven years the business was to be sold and the proceeds divided between the employees. The business finally closed in 1914.

Shudehill

It was referred to in the 1554 Court Leet Records when the highway had become blocked. In the 1650 plan of Manchester, it was a country lane with three sets of isolated cottages beyond Withy Grove. In 1569 it was spelt 'Suydehill' when Ralph Proudlove and his wife owned a property there. By the 1740s the north side had a continuous line of buildings with fields behind, whereas the south side was more open towards the end of the lane. Laurent's map fifty years later showed that the area had become completely built up.

HEN MARKET

The 1849 OS map shows a fruit market outside the Seven Stars and Mosley Arms. Later it became the Hen or Fowl Market, after moving from the Market Place in the late 1860s. Although popular with the public, it produced a number of problems. Pickpockets were at work amongst the crowds and there was concern in the 1880s about ill-treatment of the birds.

There were calls for the Society for the Prevention of Cruelty to Animals to intervene. In 1924 the Board of Agriculture made it an offence to transport fowl with their heads downwards. Letters about cruelty towards the birds were printed in the Manchester Guardian that year. They alleged that many birds were crammed together into small spaces. Others had witnessed birds being killed or half-killed by brutal methods, and buyers carrying fowl home which were still struggling in their death throes.

The Manchester RSPCA reported that proceedings had been taken against two defendants, and that their inspectors made daily visits to the market. They encouraged the public to report any incidents of ill-treatment.

Shudehill Market closed in 1948 with stall-holders being accommodated in the Market Hall. The previous year the market had been badly affected by a national outbreak of fowl pest disease. The market was a notorious site for illegal gambling and on one occasion the police made a surprise visit, arriving in a furniture van and making forty arrests.

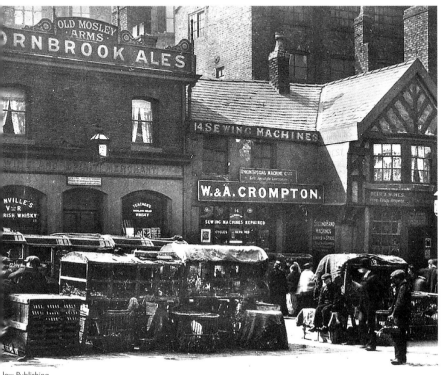

Left: The Hen Market c1910.

low Publishing

Willow Publishing

Market memories

'I wandered in at mid-day attracted by a quacking and confused bustle that promised entertainment. There was a touch of rural manners in the old folks who swarmed round the crates and cages loud with birds. A sage in a billycock hat, conspicuous for absence of teeth, was fussing round a wired box of excited ducks. He remarked they were the best ducks ever brought out of Ireland. 'Now mister' he said, putting his arm in an endearing manner within mine, 'let me sell you five. There never were birds like 'em for laying.' Meanwhile the ducks scrambled and fought, observed with interest by beshawled marketing women. One of them suddenly seized a large yellow hen by the legs and minutely inspected her. 'Now missis' shouted the owner, 'you put 'er down. It won't do good to be mauled that way.'

A huge sulky turkey stood aloft on a pile of boxes... Yet why should he be sad, having survived Christmas? Below him were other turkeys... and in a dark box all to himself a tiny goat kid. But the pride of the market was a Plymouth Rock.

Close to the fowl sellers were the miscellaneous stalls of the hangers-on. One gentleman sold spectacles and lectured on optics to passers-by, aided by a lump of polished crystal. Next door an ice-cream man anticipated the summer heats. Near to him I came across one of the few remaining open-air bookshops - a coster's barrow loaded with battered remnants of the world of letters. 'All tuppence' the bookseller declared to a rummaging throng. I dug up four volumes of the 'World', full of eighteenth century wit and elegance... They were dirt cheap for tenpence.'

Extracts from a Manchester Guardian article on Shudehill Market in 1906.

THE SHUDEHILL FOOD RIOT

Shudehill was the scene of a series of disturbances caused by four years of food scarcity and resulting high prices. In Manchester the problem was aggravated by the regulation of inhabitants forced to have their corn ground at the School Mills which could not cope with the demands of the growing population. Millers and corn-dealers were accused of profiteering.

On Tuesday 7th June 1757, two women protesters overturned sacks of potatoes which were gathered up by others. Another group went to the Meal House where they plundered the food stores while others turned over a cart coming to market at Ardwick Green. Finding they were not opposed, they raided a bread shop at Hyde's Cross before going to the Dungeon on Salford Bridge where two of their group had been held, and managed to free them. Later in the day James Bayley, the High Sheriff, arrived with an assortment of troops and volunteers to restore peace to the streets. Bayley received a letter demanding a fair price for provisions, otherwise protesters threatened to destroy his house and garden.

Then the following November, as frustrations grew throughout the population, there was an even more serious disturbance which resulted in deaths and injuries to soldiers and rioters. Considerable numbers gathered to protest on Saturday 12th November, then the following Tuesday a large group of men from Oldham, Saddleworth, Ashton and other districts marched to Manchester, destroying a corn mill at Clayton on their way.

Keith Warrender

Plaque on the corner of Shudehill and Nicholas Croft.

At Shudehill they were confronted by the military led again by James Bayley. He urged the crowd to leave the market but the 900 protesters ransacked market stalls and threw stones at the soldiers, killing one of them and injuring nine others.

The protesters wrongly thought that the military, composed of about 90 old soldiers, would not retaliate but they opened fire, killing one person. This did not stop the crowd advancing and a further three were shot dead, including a boy who had been watching the incident, perched in a tree. Another fifteen were injured and taken to the Infirmary. The crowd then dispersed but re-assembled, doing damage to mills and property just outside the town. A further group of two hundred men went in the evening to the Dungeon at Salford Bridge to try to release one of their fellow protesters. In order to prevent further unrest and bloodshed, the constables released the prisoner.

Military reinforcements were brought into Manchester to restore law and order, including a regiment of Dragoons from York and two companies of the Earl of Hulme's Derby Foot Regiment. There was also an appeal by the Earl of Warrington at Dunham for his farmers and flour dealers to make more bread available on reasonable terms. Tim Bobbin, the Lancashire poet and caricaturist, produced a pamphlet that year on the incident entitled 'Truth in a Mask, or the Shudehill Fight'. Two years later an Act was passed which freed citizens from having to use the School Mills.

163

Manchester Food Riots

The 1757 Shudehill 'Food Fight' is perhaps the best known but there had been a number of other incidents in Manchester where people protested about the price and availability of basic foodstuffs.

● In July 1762 a group from Oldham, Saddleworth and Ashton came to Manchester and caused damage to houses, warehouses and traders' goods. They left a letter saying they had agreed to stand by each other and were prepared to be hanged or starved to death, rather than see their children cry out for food. They also threatened to burn down houses and bring bloodshed to 'Shul de Hill' (Shudehill). The local constables offered a fifty-pound reward to anyone who could name the protesters.

● In 1795 the houses of unpopular grain merchants were attacked, with windows broken and furniture damaged. Public houses were ordered to close at 7pm and everyone had to be off the streets by 9pm.

● Troops were called in to disperse crowds who assembled following a dispute over potatoes in 1796.

● Following the food riots between 1797 and 1799, soup kitchens were set up to feed the needy.

● In April 1812 there was more commotion at Shudehill Market, mainly by women, protesting over the high price of potatoes which were the staple diet of many. In their frustration at the situation they seized produce from the market stalls. The military were called in and several protesters arrested.

● In June 1812 a food riot was stopped after the authorities agreed to reduce the price of potatoes from 15s to 8s per load. The cavalry had to restore law and order, and farmers sought protection from the magistrates to bring their produce to market.

● During the Bread Riots of 1822 a mill near Fountain Street was burned down.

● Spinners demonstrated in 1831 over low wages and the scarcity of foodstuffs at reasonable prices.

Spring Alley

There was a public pump here supplementing the cisterns which held rain water. The alley was in existence by 1784 when it was named amongst the streets to be cleansed and lit. A notice in the Manchester Mercury 4th September 1792, reported that Mary Spencer of Spring Alley had eloped and her husband was not responsible for her debts. Ann O'Neil and Mary M'Ginty, both well-known to the police, were at court charged with annoying passers-by in Spring Alley and Nicholas Croft on a Saturday afternoon in July 1903. They were fined 21s and costs. O'Neil had been convicted 167 times and M'Ginty128.

Manchester Libraries, Information and Archives

Mr and Mrs Morten ran a bookstall in Shudehill between 1918 and 1960.

Market stalls, Shudehill 1975.

WELLINGTON HOTEL

The hotel, which stood on Nicholas Croft, was earlier known in 1772 as 'The Two Sawyers' and then by 1779 'The Sawyers Arms'. The hotel was said to be popular with handloom weavers who nicknamed it 'The Sorrows Arms'. By 1829 there was a coach service from here to parts of Yorkshire, and, in 1860, an omnibus service ran from here every hour to the New Inn, Harpurhey.

There are references to the Sawyer's Arms up to 1838 when a land sale was held there. The earliest mention of the Wellington Hotel came in 1840 when a notice in the Manchester Guardian offered £2 reward for the recovery of six silver spoons and sugar tongs reported as missing from the premises. In November 1880 Irish Nationalists held a meeting at the hotel to make arrangements

Charles Parnell MP

supported his efforts to 'free the land of Ireland'. That evening Parnell and O'Connor attended a packed, enthusiastic meeting of the Land League at the Free Trade Hall.

Parnell, leader of the Irish Parliamentary Party, was jailed in 1882 for his vociferous support of the Irish Land League which campaigned to help poor tenant farmers. He was regarded as the person who guided the nation to Irish independence, and was an important influence in the British Parliament with the selection of Gladstone as Prime Minister. Parnell's political career ended following revelations of his affair with Katharine O'Shea. Thomas O'Connor was an MP for fifty years and Father of the House of Commons. The Irish National Club was formed at the Hotel in 1882.

The hotel was the venue in May 1887 for a meeting to raise four million pounds for the proposed Manchester Ship Canal. Thomas Barker, a tea merchant and victualler, ran the hotel with his wife from 1866 for about thirty years until his death in 1893. Barker had extended and improved the buildings during his ownership. It was in close proximity to Smithfield Market, and many of the main warehouses and other businesses.

to establish the 'Parnell Defence Fund'. This was in support of the influential MP Charles Parnell who laid the beginnings of Irish Independence. The following April, Parnell (1846-1891) and Thomas O'Connor (1848-1929) stayed here during their visit to the city. After arriving at Victoria Station they were accompanied by several thousand supporters to the hotel. It was planned that Parnell would make a speech to the crowd from a window but he was too exhausted. Instead he met with a deputation from the Democratic League of Great Britain and Ireland who

By 1911, the hotel was managed by Ester Earnshaw with nine members of staff. The licensee, Irene Priest, was in court in 1945 after refusing to serve ten large glasses of brandy and whisky to an official who said he was from the local Food and Drugs Department. He claimed it was for analytical purposes but did not produce official proof of identity. In her defence, Mrs Priest had heard of a recent case of someone being prosecuted for posing as an Excise officer, and also she didn't have enough stock to give to him. The court established that the man was genuine and she was fined £2 for obstructing an official in the execution of his duty.

Because of its location, the hotel did not have a back door which meant that the owners had to plan carefully that the swill bins were not coming out at the same time as customers entered the hotel.

It had always been a popular eating-house, and an elegant coloured folding menu had been preserved at the hotel from a banquet of the Collegiate Church ward of the Liberal Association in 1880. The guests were treated to a feast of soup, salmon, turbot, mushrooms, sweetbreads, saddle of mutton, roast beef, duckling, spring chicken, ham, plum pudding, dessert and a selection of wines. In the 1940s there used to be the Douro Vaults next door to the hotel with strangely-shaped rooms. The hotel was a popular meeting place for ex-servicemen's organisations such as the Guards, the Argylls and the Marines.

MR JOHNSON'S HOUSE

This was the residence of Thomas Johnson, a manufacturer of silk and cotton handkerchiefs. His father is thought to have built the house which was featured on Casson and Berry's 1746 map. In 1772, Thomas was listed as a check manufacturer and printer and was Borough Reeve of Manchester in 1783.

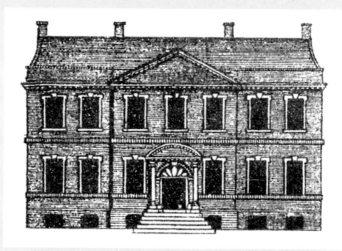

Following their annual parade at Dawson Street in 1798, the Manchester and Salford Light Horse Volunteers, along with the constables, borough reeves and gentlemen of the town went in procession to High Street and gathered outside Johnson's house to be presented with their regimental colours and royal standard. Johnson was the uncle of the colonel of the Volunteers.

Johnson Street, which was off Cannon Street, was named after him. He was a supporter of the establishment of Sunday schools, and vice-president of the local committee of the Sunday School Movement which was seen as a way of spreading literacy and moral values amongst the poor, and to keep them away from crime.

Kaiserman Collection

Collier's (right) on the corner of High Street and Cannon Street.

THOMAS COLLIER AND CO.

The firm of RT Collier on High Street was established in 1857 by Thomas Collier with his brother Richard, and Charles Bentley. They were smallware dealers, haberdashers and general merchants with another smallware business at Radcliffe. In 1871 the business was split, with Thomas and Charles continuing at High Street and Richard taking over at Radcliffe.

Thomas Collier (1831-1897) began in business as a draper in Macclesfield and the business at 33 High Street became one of the largest of its kind, with eighteen departments, including wools, dyed goods and flannels. They also had a company in Australia.

Collier lived in Broughton for over twenty-five years and was nominated as a Liberal councillor in 1874, but was not successful. He was a prominent Wesleyan, attending Higher Broughton Wesleyan Methodist Church where he was the Sunday School Superintendent for 25 years. In 1874, He presided over meetings of the

Wesleyan Foreign Missions at the Oldham Street Chapel in 1881.

By 1885 he had moved to Alderley Edge where he helped to form the local Liberal Association, and became a Cheshire County Councillor and JP. He was also the chairman of the Manchester Trust Ltd based in Manchester. Two hundred and fifty employees from his company attended his funeral, and a stained-glass window was made in his memory at the Wesleyan church in Higher Broughton. He left an estate valued at today's equivalent of £26 million. His daughter Dame Frances Mary Ryall was married to the eminent cancer surgeon Sir Charles Ryall.

Thomas's son, Frederick, ran the business until his death in 1926 when the business began to experience financial problems. It went into liquidation in 1930, and about six hundred people crowded into a creditors' meeting at the Memorial Hall, Albert Square. It was so packed that some had to stand outside in the square.

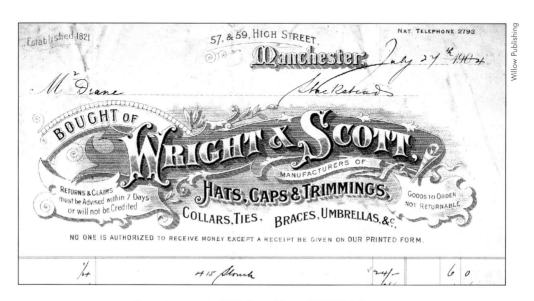

Ornate letterhead of Wright and Scott 57-59 High Street.
After 1910 they amalgamated with Smeal and Booth before
going into liquidation in 1940.

APPENDIX

Clubs in the 'Lost District'

Card Club, 23a New Cannon Street
Carina, 5 Greenwood Street
Chanteclaire, 11 Peel Street
City Centre, 11 Cromford Court
Cromford Club, Cromford Court
Drake's Drum Coffee Bar, Marsden Square
John Peel, 5 Peel Street
Magic Village, 11 Cromford Court, previously The Jigsaw and Cavern Club
Moulin Rouge, 22 Marsden Square
Pigalle Casino Club, 10/14 New Brown Street
Rails Discotheque, 66 Cannon Street
Rooster, 7 Peel Street
Stork Club, 19 Palace Street
Thatched House Pub Jazz Club
Wilton Club, 9/11 New Cannon Street

The 'Lost District' before demolition: On the lower left, the white buildings of the Printworks, previously known as Kemsley House then Maxwell House on Withy Grove leading up to Shudehill. Centre, Cannon Street up to High Street. Right, Market Street with the old Lewis's store at the top on the right.

INDEX

172

Keith Warrender

ACKNOWLEDGEMENTS

With special thanks to Chris Makepeace for providing the Introduction, photographs and advice, and to the following for their invaluable help:
Peter and David Allman, Alex Britton, Roy Bullock, David Crean, David Hilton, David Kaiserman, Chris Makepeace, James Palmes, Pauline Pitt, Dr Michael Powell, Peter Ross, Helen Webster, Ralph Manners Wood and Terry Wyke.

Also the helpful assistance of Bonhams, Bury Archives, British Library London, Chetham's Library, Congleton Museum, Manchester Archives, Greater Manchester Museum of Transport, Malcolm Ross & Sons Ltd, National Portrait Gallery, Salford Local History Library and Trafford Local Studies Library Finally, grateful thanks to David Hilton, Cynthia Hollingworth and Judith Warrender for checking the text.

Further Information
Blitz Britain - Manchester and Salford, by Graham Phythian
CP Scott, The Making of the Manchester Guardian, published 1946
Gang War, by Peter Walsh
Hell is a City - film (DVD)
History of the County Palatine & Duchy of Lancaster, by Edward Baines
In Plain Sight: The Life and Lies of Jimmy Saville, by Alan Davies
Lancashire Non-Conformity, by Benjamin Nightingale
Levenshulme History, Then & Now, (website) by George Nixon (Hell is a City)
Life Between the Lines, by John Izbicki
Mad Frank's Underworld History of Britain, by Frankie Fraser & James Morten
Manchester Fifty Years Ago, by JT Slugg
Manchester in the Dark, the Cinemas of Central Manchester & Ardwick Green, by Derek Southall
Manchester of Yesterday, by THG Stevens
Manchester Region History Review journal, various
Manchester Streets and Manchester Men, by T Swindells
New Manchester Guide (1815)
Origins of Street Names in the City Centre of Manchester, by LD Bradshaw
Our Blitz, Red Sky Over Manchester, by Kemsley Newspapers
Sit Down! Listen To This! The Roger Eagle Story, by Bill Sykes
The Irish Giant, by G Frankcom & JH Musgrave
The Life of Charles Stewart Parnell, by R Barry O'Brien
The Manchester Carriage and Tramways Company, by Edward Gray
The Voice of the People, John Doherty, by RG Kirby & AE Musson
Underground Manchester, by Keith Warrender